THIS BOOK

BELONGS TO

....

I can't tell you how grateful I am that you decided to read my book. My most heartfelt thanks that you took time out of your life to choose my work and I hope you find benefit within these pages.

There are so many books available today that offer similar content so that makes it even more humbling that you decided to buying mine.

Tell me what you thought! I am eager to hear your opinion and ideas on what you read as are others who are looking for a good book to buy. Leave a review on Amazon.com so others can benefit from your wisdom!

With much thanks.

Table of Contents

SUMMARY

The Enchanting World of C2C Crochet: C2C crochet, short for corner-to-corner crochet, is a popular and enchanting technique that has taken the crochet world by storm. This unique method involves working diagonally from one corner of a project to the opposite corner, creating a stunning and intricate design. With its versatility and endless possibilities, C2C crochet has captured the hearts of crocheters of all skill levels.

One of the most appealing aspects of C2C crochet is its simplicity. The technique primarily uses double crochet stitches, making it accessible to beginners while still offering a challenge for more experienced crocheters. By working in a diagonal direction, the pattern gradually expands, resulting in a beautiful and symmetrical design. This gradual increase in stitches also allows for easy customization, as crocheters can easily adjust the size of their project by adding or subtracting rows.

The enchanting world of C2C crochet offers a wide range of possibilities for creativity. From simple geometric patterns to intricate images and motifs, the design options are virtually limitless. Crocheters can create stunning blankets, scarves, shawls, and even garments using this technique. The ability to incorporate different colors and yarn types further enhances the versatility of C2C crochet, allowing for endless combinations and unique designs.

One of the most exciting aspects of C2C crochet is the ability to create stunning pixelated images. By using a graph or chart, crocheters can recreate intricate pictures and designs with ease. This technique is particularly popular for creating character-themed blankets, such as those featuring beloved cartoon characters or iconic movie scenes. The pixelated effect adds a touch of whimsy and nostalgia to the finished project, making it a cherished keepsake for years to come.

In addition to its aesthetic appeal, C2C crochet also offers practical benefits. The diagonal construction of the stitches creates a dense and sturdy fabric, making it ideal for items that require durability, such as blankets and bags. The technique also lends itself well to colorwork, allowing for seamless color changes and clean edges. This makes it a popular choice for crocheters who enjoy experimenting with different color combinations and creating visually striking projects.

The enchanting world of C2C crochet is not limited to traditional patterns and designs. Many crocheters have taken this technique to new heights by incorporating other crochet stitches and techniques into their C2C projects. This fusion of styles and techniques adds an extra layer of complexity and visual interest to the finished piece. From lace-like motifs to textured stitches,

Traversing from One Corner to Another in Crochet Canvas: Traversing from one corner to another in crochet canvas involves moving across the fabric in a diagonal direction, starting from one corner and ending at the opposite corner. This technique is commonly used in crochet projects to create various patterns and designs.

To begin traversing from one corner to another, you first need to identify the starting corner and the ending corner of your crochet canvas. The starting corner is usually the bottom left or bottom right corner, while the ending corner is the top left or top right corner, depending on your project.

Once you have determined the starting and ending corners, you can begin the process of traversing. Start by inserting your crochet hook into the first stitch at the starting corner. This stitch will serve as your anchor point for the diagonal movement across the fabric.

Next, you will need to decide on the direction of your diagonal movement. This can be either from bottom left to top right or from bottom right to top left, depending on your preference and the desired pattern. For example, if you want to create a chevron pattern, you would typically move from bottom left to top right.

To move diagonally, you will need to work your way across the fabric by inserting your crochet hook into the next stitch in a diagonal direction. This means that instead of inserting your hook directly into the next stitch in a straight line, you will insert it slightly to the left or right, depending on the direction of your diagonal movement.

Continue this process of inserting your crochet hook into the next stitch in a diagonal direction until you reach the ending corner of your crochet canvas. Along the way, you will be creating stitches that form a diagonal line across the fabric, gradually moving from one corner to another.

It is important to maintain an even tension and consistent stitch size throughout the traversal process to ensure that your fabric remains flat and the pattern is evenly distributed. Take your time and pay attention to each stitch as you work your way across the fabric.

Once you reach the ending corner, you can finish off your traversal by securing the last stitch and weaving in any loose ends. You can then continue with your crochet project, incorporating the traversed diagonal line into your desired pattern or design.

Traversing from one corner to another in crochet canvas can add depth and visual interest to your projects. It allows you to create unique patterns and designs that are not possible with traditional straight-line crochet techniques. With practice and experimentation, you can master this technique and use it to enhance your crochet creations.

Inviting You to Explore, Create, and Innovate with C2C Crochet: We are thrilled to extend an invitation to you to embark on a journey of exploration, creation, and innovation with C2C Crochet. C2C, or Corner-to-Corner, crochet is a versatile and exciting technique that allows you to create stunning and intricate designs using simple stitches.

With C2C Crochet, the possibilities are endless. Whether you are a seasoned crocheter or just starting out, this technique offers a whole new world of creativity to explore. By working diagonally from one corner to another, you can create beautiful patterns, images, and even intricate tapestries.

One of the most exciting aspects of C2C Crochet is the ability to incorporate color into your designs. By using different colored yarns, you can create stunning gradients, bold contrasts, or even intricate pixelated images. The technique allows you to easily switch between colors, giving you the freedom to experiment and create unique and eye-catching designs.

Not only does C2C Crochet offer endless creative possibilities, but it also provides a sense of accomplishment and satisfaction. As you work on your project, you will see your design come to life, row by row. The repetitive nature of the stitches can be soothing and meditative, allowing you to relax and unwind while creating something beautiful.

Furthermore, C2C Crochet is a technique that can be easily adapted to suit your personal style and preferences. Whether you prefer working with fine yarns and delicate stitches or chunky yarns and bold designs, C2C Crochet can be tailored to your liking. You can also experiment with different stitch patterns, textures, and embellishments to add your own personal touch to your creations.

In addition to the creative aspect, C2C Crochet also offers a sense of community and connection. There are numerous online communities, forums, and social media groups dedicated to C2C Crochet, where you can connect with fellow enthusiasts, share your work, and seek inspiration. These communities provide a supportive and encouraging environment, where you can learn from others, exchange ideas, and celebrate each other's achievements.

So, whether you are looking to expand your crochet skills, unleash your creativity, or simply find a new hobby to enjoy, we invite you to explore, create, and innovate with C2C Crochet. Join us on this exciting journey and discover the endless possibilities that await you in the world of C2C Crochet.

How to Navigate Through This Creative Crochet Adventure of C2C Crochet: Welcome to the exciting world of C2C crochet! This creative crochet adventure will take you on a journey of creating beautiful and intricate designs using the Corner-to-Corner technique. Whether you are a beginner or an experienced crocheter, this guide will help you navigate through the process and create stunning C2C crochet projects.

Firstly, let's understand what C2C crochet is all about. Corner-to-Corner crochet is a technique that involves working diagonally from one corner of your project to the opposite corner. This technique creates a unique textured fabric with a pixelated look, making it perfect for creating detailed images, patterns, and designs.

To start your C2C crochet adventure, you will need a few essential tools and materials. These include a crochet hook, yarn of your choice, and a pattern or graph to follow. The size of your crochet hook and the weight of your yarn will depend on the desired outcome of your project. Thicker yarn and larger hooks will create a larger and more textured fabric, while thinner yarn and smaller hooks will result in a finer and more delicate fabric.

Once you have gathered your materials, it's time to dive into the world of C2C crochet. The first step is to learn the basic C2C stitch. This stitch involves creating a series of double crochet stitches in a diagonal direction, increasing or decreasing the number of stitches in each row to create the desired shape and size.

To create a C2C project, you will need to follow a pattern or graph. A graph is a visual representation of the design you want to create, with each square representing a stitch. Each row of the graph corresponds to a row of stitches in your project. By following the graph and changing colors as needed, you can create intricate images and patterns.

As you progress through your C2C crochet adventure, you will encounter various techniques and tips to enhance your projects. These include changing colors, carrying yarn, and creating borders. Changing colors allows you to create detailed images and patterns by switching yarn colors at specific points in your project. Carrying yarn involves carrying the unused yarn along the back of your work, reducing the number of ends to weave in. Adding a border to your C2C project gives it a finished and polished look.

Remember, practice makes perfect! As with any new skill, it may take some time and practice to master C2C crochet. Start with simple patterns and gradually work your way up to more complex designs.

The Basics of Corner to Corner Stitching: Corner to corner stitching, also known as C2C stitching, is a popular crochet technique that creates a textured and visually appealing fabric. This technique involves working diagonally from one corner of a project to the opposite corner, using a combination of double crochet stitches and chain stitches.

To begin a corner to corner project, you will need to start with a chain of stitches. The number of chains will depend on the size of the project you are working on. Once you have your chain, you will work your first row by making double crochet stitches into each chain stitch.

After completing the first row, you will begin to increase the size of your project by adding additional stitches to each row. To do this, you will work a series of double crochet stitches into the chain spaces of the previous row. This creates a diagonal line of stitches that gradually increases in size.

As you continue to work your corner to corner project, you will notice that the fabric begins to take on a triangular shape. This is because each row is slightly longer than the previous one, due to the increases made at the beginning of each row. This gradual increase in size creates a unique and visually interesting texture.

One of the benefits of corner to corner stitching is its versatility. This technique can be used to create a wide range of projects, from blankets and scarves to dishcloths and bags. The diagonal lines created by the stitches can be used to create intricate patterns and designs, making it a popular choice for those looking to add visual interest to their crochet projects.

Corner to corner stitching is also a great technique for using up leftover yarn. Because each row increases in size, you can easily adjust the size of your project based on the amount of yarn you have available. This makes it a cost-effective option for those looking to make the most of their yarn stash.

While corner to corner stitching may seem intimidating at first, it is actually a relatively simple technique to master. Once you understand the basic stitches and increases, you can easily create stunning projects using this method. There are also many tutorials and patterns available online that can help guide you through the process.

In conclusion, corner to corner stitching is a versatile and visually appealing crochet technique that can be used to create a wide range of projects. Whether you are a beginner or an experienced crocheter, this technique is worth exploring. With a little practice and creativity, you can create beautiful and unique pieces using the corner to corner stitching method.

Decoding the Pixel Art of C2C Crochet:

A Comprehensive Guide to Understanding and Creating Intricate Designs

Introduction:

C2C (corner-to-corner) crochet has gained immense popularity in recent years due to its ability to create stunning pixel art designs. This technique involves working diagonally from one corner of a square to the opposite corner, using a combination of double crochet stitches and color changes to create intricate patterns. In this guide, we will delve into the world of C2C crochet and explore the techniques, tools, and tips necessary to decode and create pixel art designs.

Understanding the Basics:

Before diving into the pixel art aspect of C2C crochet, it is essential to grasp the fundamentals of this technique. C2C crochet involves working in a grid-like pattern, with each square representing a stitch. By increasing or decreasing stitches at the beginning or end of each row, you can create a diagonal shape that forms the basis of C2C crochet. Understanding how to read and follow a C2C crochet chart is crucial for decoding pixel art designs.

Decoding Pixel Art Designs:

Pixel art designs are essentially images that have been broken down into individual pixels, each representing a specific color. Decoding these designs involves translating each pixel into a corresponding stitch and color in C2C crochet. This can be achieved by using a C2C crochet chart, which provides a visual representation of the design and indicates the color changes required for each stitch.

Tools and Materials:

To successfully decode and create pixel art designs in C2C crochet, you will need a few essential tools and materials. These include a crochet hook, yarn in various colors, a C2C crochet chart, and a tapestry needle for weaving in ends. It is important to choose a yarn that is suitable for C2C crochet, as it should be soft, durable, and have good stitch definition to showcase the intricate pixel art designs.

Tips and Techniques:

Decoding and creating pixel art designs in C2C crochet can be a challenging task, but with the right techniques and tips, it becomes an enjoyable and rewarding experience. Here are a few tips to help you along the way:

Start with simple designs: As a beginner, it is advisable to start with simpler pixel art designs that have fewer color changes. This will help you understand the technique and build your confidence before tackling more complex designs.

Reading and Creating Graphgans of C2C Crochet: Reading and creating graphgans of C2C crochet is a fascinating and creative endeavor that allows crochet enthusiasts to explore a unique and visually stunning technique. Graphgans, short for graph afghans, are crochet projects that are worked using a grid-like pattern, where each square on the grid represents a stitch. This technique is particularly popular in the world of C2C (corner-to-corner) crochet, which involves working diagonally from one corner of the project to the other.

To begin with, reading graphgans requires a basic understanding of crochet stitches and terminology. Each square on the graph represents a specific stitch, such as a single crochet, double crochet, or even a color change. By following the graph, crocheters can create intricate and detailed designs, ranging from simple geometric patterns to elaborate images of animals, landscapes, or even pop culture references.

One of the key advantages of working with graphgans is the ability to create highly detailed and realistic designs. The grid-like pattern allows for precise placement of stitches, resulting in a finished project that closely resembles the intended image. This level of detail can be particularly impressive when working with images that have a lot of shading or intricate patterns.

Creating graphgans of C2C crochet involves a combination of following a graph and using color changes to bring the design to life. Crocheters can choose to work with a single color throughout the project or incorporate multiple colors to add depth and dimension to the design. Color changes are typically done by joining a new yarn color at the appropriate stitch and carrying the unused color along the back of the work. This technique allows for seamless transitions between colors and creates a clean and professional-looking finished project.

While reading and creating graphgans of C2C crochet may seem daunting at first, there are plenty of resources available to help beginners get started. Online tutorials, video demonstrations, and written patterns can provide step-by-step instructions and guidance on how to read and follow a graph. Additionally, there are software programs and apps that can convert images into graph patterns, making it easier to create custom designs.

In conclusion, reading and creating graphgans of C2C crochet is a rewarding and creative endeavor that allows crochet enthusiasts to explore their artistic side. With the ability to create highly detailed and realistic designs, graphgans offer a unique way to showcase one's crochet skills and create beautiful and personalized projects.

Materials and Tools Essential for C2C Crochet: When it comes to C2C crochet, there are a few essential materials and tools that you will need to have on hand in order to successfully complete your project. C2C, or corner-to-corner, crochet is a popular technique that involves working diagonally from one corner of a project to the opposite corner, creating a textured and visually appealing design.

First and foremost, you will need a suitable yarn for your C2C crochet project. The type of yarn you choose will depend on the desired outcome of your project, as well as personal preference. It is important to select a yarn that is appropriate for the size of your crochet hook and that will provide the desired drape and texture for your finished piece. Some popular yarn choices for C2C crochet include acrylic, cotton, and wool blends.

In addition to yarn, you will also need a crochet hook. The size of the hook will depend on the weight of the yarn you are using and the tension you want to achieve. It is important to choose a hook that is comfortable for you to hold and work with for extended periods of time. Many C2C crochet projects require a larger hook size to create a looser and more open stitch pattern.

Another essential tool for C2C crochet is a pair of scissors. You will need scissors to cut your yarn at the end of each row or when changing colors. It is important to have a sharp pair of scissors that can easily cut through the yarn without fraying or damaging it.

Additionally, you may find it helpful to have a tapestry needle or yarn needle on hand. This tool is used for weaving in loose ends and finishing off your project. A tapestry needle has a large eye and a blunt tip, making it easy to thread and maneuver through your stitches.

Lastly, it is important to have a clear and concise pattern or chart for your C2C crochet project. This will serve as your guide and help you keep track of your stitches and color changes. Whether you prefer written instructions or visual charts, having a pattern will ensure that you stay on track and achieve the desired design.

In conclusion, C2C crochet requires a few essential materials and tools to successfully complete your project. These include suitable yarn, a crochet hook, scissors, a tapestry needle, and a clear pattern or chart. By having these items on hand, you will be well-equipped to create beautiful and intricate C2C crochet designs.

Working the Basic C2C Stitch: To work the basic C2C (corner-to-corner) stitch, you will need a crochet hook and yarn of your choice. This stitch is commonly used in crochet projects to create a textured and visually appealing fabric. It is called C2C because you work diagonally from one corner to the opposite corner of your project.

To begin, make a slip knot and place it on your crochet hook. Then, chain 6 stitches. This will serve as your foundation chain.

Next, double crochet (dc) into the fourth chain from your hook. This will create your first block. To double crochet, yarn over, insert your hook into the designated stitch, yarn over again, and pull through the stitch. You should have three loops on your hook. Yarn over once more and pull through the first two loops on your hook. Yarn over again and pull through the remaining two loops. This completes one double crochet stitch.

Now, you will continue to double crochet into the next two chains of your foundation chain. This will create a total of three double crochet stitches, forming your first row.

To start the second row, chain 6 stitches. This chain will act as your turning chain. Turn your work so that you are now working in the opposite direction.

Next, double crochet into the fourth chain from your hook, just like you did in the first row. This will create your first block in the second row. Double crochet into the next two chains of your turning chain to complete the row.

To continue working the C2C stitch, you will repeat the steps for the second row. Each row will have one additional block compared to the previous row. This creates the diagonal effect of the C2C stitch.

Continue working rows in this manner until you reach your desired size or until your pattern instructs you to stop. Remember to always chain 6 stitches at the beginning of each row as your turning chain.

Once you have completed your C2C project, you can finish it off by fastening off your yarn. Cut the yarn, leaving a tail, and pull it through the last loop on your hook to secure it.

The C2C stitch is versatile and can be used to create a variety of projects such as blankets, scarves, and even garments. Experiment with different yarn colors and textures to create unique and personalized items. With practice, you will become more comfortable with the C2C stitch and be able to incorporate it into your crochet repertoire.

Increasing and Decreasing in C2C Crochet: C2C crochet, also known as corner-to-corner crochet, is a popular technique used to create a variety of projects such as blankets, scarves, and even garments. One of the unique features of C2C crochet is the ability to create both increasing and decreasing sections within the same project.

When working on a C2C crochet project, the increasing section refers to the part where the number of stitches is gradually increasing, resulting in a larger piece. This is typically done by adding one or more stitches to each row or round. The increasing section is often used to create the diagonal shape that is characteristic of C2C crochet.

To start the increasing section, you begin with a small number of stitches, usually three, and work a series of double crochet stitches into each stitch of the previous row or round. As you progress, you will notice that the number of stitches in each row or round increases, creating a triangular shape. This can be achieved by either adding stitches at the beginning or end of each row or round, or by working multiple stitches into the same stitch.

On the other hand, the decreasing section in C2C crochet refers to the part where the number of stitches is gradually decreasing, resulting in a smaller piece. This is often done to shape the project or create a specific design element. The decreasing section is typically used to create the opposite diagonal shape, completing the overall design.

To start the decreasing section, you begin with a larger number of stitches and gradually decrease the number of stitches in each row or round. This can be achieved by skipping stitches or working stitches together. By doing so, you will notice that the number of stitches in each row or round decreases, creating a triangular shape in the opposite direction.

Both the increasing and decreasing sections in C2C crochet require careful attention to stitch placement and counting. It is important to keep track of the number of stitches in each row or round to ensure that the desired shape is achieved. Additionally, it is crucial to maintain consistent tension throughout the project to ensure an even and professional finish.

In conclusion, C2C crochet offers the versatility to create both increasing and decreasing sections within the same project. By mastering these techniques, you can create stunning designs and unique patterns that showcase the beauty of C2C crochet.

Whether you are a beginner or an experienced crocheter, exploring the possibilities of increasing and decreasing in C2C crochet can open up a world of creative opportunities.

Managing Color Changes and Tails of C2C Crochet:

C2C crochet, also known as corner-to-corner crochet, is a popular technique that creates a textured and visually appealing fabric. One of the challenges that crocheters often face when working on C2C projects is managing color changes and dealing with the tails that are left behind.

Color changes in C2C crochet are necessary to create the intricate patterns and designs that make this technique so unique. However, it can be tricky to seamlessly transition from one color to another without leaving any gaps or loose ends. To manage color changes effectively, it is important to plan ahead and have a clear idea of the color scheme you want to achieve.

One technique that can be used to manage color changes is the carry-along method. This involves carrying the unused color along the back of the work while crocheting with the new color. By doing this, you can avoid cutting the yarn and creating unnecessary tails. However, it is important to be mindful of the tension and not pull the carried yarn too tightly, as this can distort the fabric.

Another method to manage color changes is the invisible join technique. This involves joining the new color with a slip stitch and then weaving in the tail as you continue crocheting. This creates a seamless transition between colors and eliminates the need for cutting and weaving in multiple tails. However, it requires some practice to master the invisible join and ensure that it is truly invisible.

When it comes to dealing with the tails left behind from color changes, there are a few options. One option is to weave in the tails as you go. This involves crocheting over the tails as you work, securing them in place and minimizing the need for additional finishing work. However, this method can be challenging if the tails are too short or if the fabric is too dense.

Another option is to leave longer tails and weave them in at the end. This allows for more flexibility in terms of securing the tails and ensures that they are hidden within the fabric. However, it does require additional time and effort to weave in the tails neatly and securely.

Regardless of the method you choose, it is important to take the time to weave in the tails properly. This involves using a yarn needle to thread the tail through the stitches of the fabric, going back and forth to secure it in place.

Tips for Clean and Defined Pixel Squares of C2C Crochet: C2C crochet, also known as corner-to-corner crochet, is a popular technique that allows you to create beautiful pixelated designs. However, achieving clean and defined pixel squares can sometimes be a challenge. Here are some tips to help you achieve the best results:

1. Choose the right yarn: The type of yarn you use can greatly affect the outcome of your C2C crochet project. Opt for a yarn that has good stitch definition and is not too fuzzy. This will help to create crisp and well-defined pixel squares.

2. Use the right hook size: The size of your crochet hook can also impact the clarity of your pixel squares. If your hook is too small, your stitches may be too tight and the squares may appear cramped. On the other hand, if your hook is too large, your stitches may be too loose and the squares may look sloppy. Experiment with different hook sizes to find the one that gives you the desired result.

3. Maintain consistent tension: Consistent tension is key to achieving clean and defined pixel squares. Try to keep your tension even throughout your project. If your tension varies, it can result in squares that are different sizes or shapes, which can affect the overall appearance of your design.

4. Block your squares: Blocking is a technique used to shape and smooth out your crochet work. After completing each square, wet block it by gently washing it and then pinning it into shape. This will help to even out any inconsistencies and give your squares a polished look.

5. Pay attention to color changes: C2C crochet often involves changing colors to create the pixelated design. To ensure clean and defined squares, pay attention to how you carry your yarn when changing colors. Avoid carrying the yarn too tightly or too loosely, as this can distort the shape of your squares. Take the time to weave in any loose ends neatly to maintain a tidy appearance.

6. Practice good stitch placement: Proper stitch placement is crucial for achieving clean and defined pixel squares. Make sure to insert your hook into the correct stitch and work your stitches evenly. Avoid skipping stitches or working too loosely, as this can result in squares that are not well-defined.

7. Take your time: C2C crochet can be a time-consuming technique, especially when working on larger projects. Take your time and work at a pace that allows you to maintain consistent tension and stitch placement. Rushing through your work can lead to mistakes and less defined squares.

Cleaning and Washing Guidelines of C2C Crochet: Cleaning and washing guidelines for C2C crochet are essential to maintain the quality and longevity of your handmade item. C2C crochet, also known as corner-to-corner crochet, is a popular technique used to create beautiful and intricate designs. Whether you have made a blanket, a scarf, or any other item using this technique, it is important to know how to properly clean and care for it.

Firstly, before attempting to clean your C2C crochet item, it is crucial to read and follow any care instructions provided by the yarn manufacturer. Different types of yarn may have specific cleaning requirements, such as hand washing only or machine washable on a gentle cycle. Following these instructions will help prevent any damage to your crochet piece.

If there are no specific care instructions, it is generally recommended to hand wash your C2C crochet item. Fill a basin or sink with lukewarm water and add a mild detergent specifically designed for delicate fabrics. Gently submerge the crochet item into the water and swish it around to ensure that the detergent is evenly distributed. Avoid rubbing or scrubbing the crochet as this can cause the fibers to become tangled or stretched.

After soaking the crochet item for a few minutes, carefully drain the soapy water and refill the basin with clean lukewarm water. Rinse the crochet item by gently swishing it around in the water, ensuring that all the detergent is removed. Repeat this rinsing process until the water runs clear, indicating that all the soap has been washed away.

Once the crochet item is thoroughly rinsed, gently squeeze out any excess water. Avoid wringing or twisting the item as this can distort its shape. Instead, lay the crochet item flat on a clean towel and roll it up, pressing gently to absorb the remaining moisture. Unroll the towel and carefully reshape the crochet item to its original dimensions. Lay it flat on a dry towel or a mesh drying rack, ensuring that it is not exposed to direct sunlight or heat sources, as this can cause fading or damage to the fibers.

If your C2C crochet item is machine washable, it is important to use a gentle cycle and place it in a mesh laundry bag or pillowcase to protect it from getting tangled or stretched. Additionally, it is advisable to wash it with similar colors to prevent any color bleeding or transfer. After the wash cycle is complete, follow the same steps as mentioned above for rinsing and drying.

In terms of stain removal, it is best to address any

Quincy & Co Owl - Abyssinian

Quincy & Co Owl - Cerulean

Quincy & Co Owl - Cinnamon

Quincy & Co Owl - Huckleberry

Quincy & Co Owl - Canyon

Tools and Materials

C2C crochet requires the same tools as traditional crochet, but the following extra few items can go a long way in making the technique fun and enjoyable.

Ruler

It's helpful to use a ruler to draw a line through each row in the graph pattern as you complete it. You'll also want to do a test swatch and measure your gauge before starting a project.

Clipboard

It seems so simple, but placing your graph on a clipboard while you crochet on the couch can make it much easier to cross off the rows as you work. Less time looking for your pen means more time to crochet!

Scissors

Keep a small pair handy for switching colors and trimming ends.

Tapestry Needle

You'll want to have a tapestry needle nearby for weaving in ends. For denser, fabric-like yarns, you might find it helpful to use a sharper upholstery needle or a small crochet hook.

Bobbin Tools

When working a graph with several color changes, clothespins, binder clips or industrial clips allow you to wind off a small ball of yarn and clip it to the project or a sturdy object nearby.

Bobbin Management System

We cover bobbins a lot more later on (see Managing Yarns: Tips for Wrangling Your Yarn), but for now, just know that you'll develop your own method for keeping your separate bobbins or yarn balls organized when switching colors. Laundry baskets with holes, a shoe box with holes poked in the top, or a bottle drying rack all make inexpensive household solutions.

TIP

Before you start any of the projects in this book, make a photocopy of both the graph and the line-by-line written instructions so you can cross off each row as you complete it without writing in the book. Carefully tracking your progress row by row is a key to C2C success!

How to C2C

C2C Basics

The corner to corner crochet technique (often abbreviated C2C) is worked exactly as it sounds – diagonally from one corner of a square or rectangle to the other. C2C employs a stitch called the diagonal box stitch and it can be worked using double crochet or half double crochet stitches. While using double crochet is faster, half double crochet allows for more detailed yarn "illustrations" because each tile is smaller. The projects in this book will call out which stitch to use.

HOW TO READ A C2C PATTERN

C2C patterns usually include some combination of a graph and/or written instructions. Each pixel in a graph represents one C2C "tile". Each tile is typically made with three double crochet or half double crochet stitches. C2C blankets with designs in them are often called "graphgans", because they are an afghan made from a graph.

The patterns in this book include both a graph as well as written line-by-line instructions. You may find it faster to work predominantly from the written pattern, but I recommend checking your completed progress against the graph every few rows so you can catch any mistakes sooner rather than later (I've learned this the hard way!).

Each project begins in the lower right corner of the graph, even for left-handed crocheters. You'll increase by one tile per row (see How to Increase) until the longest row(s) of the pattern has been completed. At this point, you'll begin decreasing by one tile per row until you've reached the final tile in the upper left corner of the graph (see How to Decrease).

Each written pattern contains a lot of helpful information:

Yarn Type and Yardage: Amount is overestimated so you can create multiple working bobbins in each color.

Stitch Type: Whether the pattern calls for using a half double crochet C2C stitch or a double crochet C2C stitch.

Color Key: Bridges the visual information in the graph with the written pattern. For simplicity, each color in the written pattern is called by the brand name color. Of course, feel free to change up the color palette of each project to suit your style.

Directional Arrows: Referencing these arrows in the written pattern can be helpful tracking your progress in the graph and knowing when to increase or decrease at the beginning of a row.

Row-by-Row Instructions: How many tiles of each color to crochet.

Difficulty Level: Know what you're getting into!

Beginner: No color changes or counting.	✚ ✢ ✢
Intermediate: Few to moderate number of color changes and working bobbins/skeins.	✚ ✚ ✢
Advanced: More counting and several working bobbins/skeins at once.	✚ ✚ ✚

How to Read a Graph

SAMPLE PATTERN

◀ **Row 1 [RS]:** Coral x 1
▶ **Row 2 [WS]:** Coral x 2
◀ **Row 3:** Coral x 3
▶ **Row 4:** Coral x 1, Grey x 2, Coral x 1
◀ **Row 5:** Coral x 2, Grey x 1, Coral x 2

CORNER *(decrease at beginning of each row)*

▶ **Row 6 [WS]:** Coral x 1, Grey x 2, Coral x 1
◀ **Row 7 [RS]:** Coral x 3
▶ **Row 8:** Coral x 2
◀ **Row 9:** Coral x 1

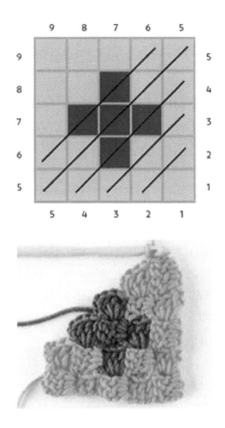

DESIGNING YOUR OWN GRAPHS

So you're ready to map out your own design? Awesome! Here are some tips for getting started.

1. Come up with a concept. Perler bead graphs, cross stitch and modern textiles can all serve as excellent C2C inspiration.

2. Determine sizing. To figure out how many tiles wide and tall your project should be to create the size you want, you need to first know your gauge. Crochet a small swatch that has six tiles per side. Measure the middle four tiles in both directions and average that number to determine the length of four tiles. Take this length and divide by 4. The resulting number is the approximate length of one tile.

Take the total desired width of your project and divide that number by the length of one tile. This number is the approximate number of tiles you should work for the width of your project. Repeat the same equation to determine the number of tiles to create your desired project length.

Example:

If 4 tiles measure 5in (12.75cm) and I want to make a blanket that is 50 x 60in (127 x 152cm):

Approximate length of one tile is 5/4 = $1^{1}/_{4}$in

Desired blanket width = 50in divided by $1^{1}/_{4}$in = 40 tiles

Desired blanket height = 60in divided by $1^{1}/_{4}$in = 48 tiles

3. *Chart it.* Even if your design only includes stripes, it's still a good idea to map it out before you get started. Grab some graph paper or head to StitchFiddle.com to design your graph based on the total number of tiles per side you determined above. Stitch Fiddle is a fantastic resource that even allows you to upload a photo and convert it to a graph, create written line-by-line instructions from your graph, and track your progress as you crochet.

How to Increase

In C2C, we refer to "increasing" as adding one tile per row. The first half of any project involves increasing at the beginning of each row. Once you have finished the longest row in the graph, you will begin decreasing at the beginning of each row.

HOW TO INCREASE USING THE DOUBLE CROCHET C2C STITCH

ROW 1:

Step 1: Ch 6

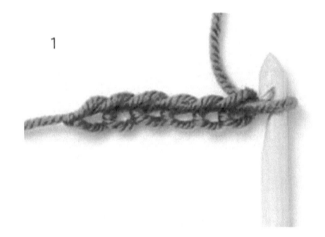

Step 2: Dc into the fourth ch from the hook

Step 3: Dc into the next 2 chs, turn

ROW 2:

Step 4: Ch 6

Step 5: Dc into the fourth ch from the hook and into the next 2 chs

Step 6: Skip the next 3 dc, then slst into the space created by ch-3 at end of tile

Step 7: Ch 3 quite tightly

Step 8: Dc 3 into the same space, turn. (1 tile made)

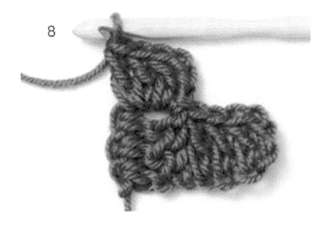

ROW 3 and beyond:

Repeat Steps 4-8 to begin each row. As rows increase in number of tiles, repeat Steps 6-8 in each remaining tile of row.

HOW TO INCREASE USING THE HALF DOUBLE CROCHET C2C STITCH

ROW 1:

Step 1: Ch 5

Step 2: Hdc into the third ch from the hook

Step 3: Hdc into the next 2 chs, turn

ROW 2:

Step 4: Ch 5

Step 5: Hdc into the fourth ch from the hook and into the next 2 chs

Step 6: Skip the next 3 hdc, then slst into the space created by ch-2 at end of tile

Step 7: Ch 2 quite tightly

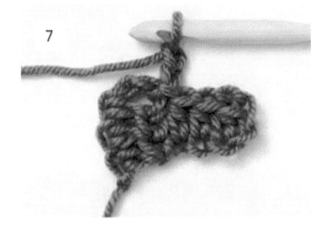

Step 8: Hdc 3 into the same space, turn. (1 tile made)

ROW 3 and beyond:

Repeat Steps 4-8 to begin each row. As rows increase in number of tiles, repeat Steps 6-8 in each remaining tile of row.

How to Decrease

The "decrease" term in C2C can be slightly confusing because it has a different effect than we think of in traditional crochet. In C2C, a decrease eliminates one tile from each row, thereby creating a flat edge. You'll work the C2C decrease stitch at the beginning of each row once you've completed the longest row in your graph.

HOW TO DECREASE USING THE DOUBLE CROCHET C2C STITCH

Step 1: Ch 1, slst into the next 3 dc

Step 2: Slst into the ch-3 turning chain

Step 3: Ch 3 quite tightly

Step 4: Dc 3 into the ch-3 turning chain of previous row

4

Repeat Steps 6-8 of the tutorial "How to Increase Using the Double Crochet C2C Stitch" in each remaining tile of row (see How to Increase).

HOW TO DECREASE USING THE HALF DOUBLE CROCHET C2C STITCH

Step 1: Ch 1, slst in the next 3 hdc

1

Step 2: Slst into the ch-2 turning chain

2

Step 3: Ch 2 quite tightly

3

Step 4: Hdc 3 into the ch-2 turning chain of previous row

4

Repeat Steps 6-8 of the "How to Increase Using the Half Double Crochet C2C Stitch" tutorial in each remaining tile of row (see How to Increase).

Changing Color

When your C2C chart or graph indicates that it's time to create a tile in a new color, you will actually begin the color change in the last yarn over of the original colored tile.

While the instructions below explain how to change colors when working in double crochet, the technique is exactly the same when using half double crochet stitches; simply work half double crochet tiles instead of double crochet tiles.

Step 1: Do not complete the last yarn over of third dc

Step 2: Instead, yarn over with the new color to complete the dc

Step 3: Skip the next 3 dc, then slst tightly into the space created by ch-3 at end of tile. Ch 3 tightly, using new color

Step 4: Using new color, work 3 dc in ch-3 sp as you usually would

Repeat Steps 1-4 each time it's necessary to change colors in the graph.

BEGINNING A ROW WITH A NEW COLOR

When changing colors at the beginning of a row, you'll do something very similar depending on whether you're working an increase or decrease tile.

> When beginning an increase row in a new color, the color change will take place in the last final yarn over of the previous row. Ch 6 with the new color and proceed as usual.

> For a decrease row, begin the row by using the previous color to slst 3 up the edge of the last tile in the previous row. Switch to new color to complete fourth slst and proceed as usual.

TIP

People often ask what the back of a C2C project will look like. The answer is that it will be an exact reflection of the front. So if your project includes words, you can expect them to appear backward on the backside of the project.

Managing Yarns

REDUCING THOSE PESKY ENDS TO WEAVE IN

Weaving in ends is often the price you pay for a spectacular C2C design, but there are a few ways to minimize your effort. For one, it's not necessary to cut the original colored yarn after each color change. Keeping it attached whenever possible will allow you to pick it up again if necessary in the next row.

Similarly, crocheting over the tails of yarn you do cut will significantly reduce the ends to weave in. My rule of thumb is that if the color of the tail matches either the tiles below it or the tiles I'm crocheting above it, then I'll work over the tail. If for example though, a tail is dark and the tiles below and above it are light, I wouldn't crochet over it because it wouldn't disappear enough into the light-colored yarn. In this case, I'd leave the dark tail to weave into a dark tile later on. At some points in a pattern, you may use several different colors in one row. This is when it can be helpful to have a few working skeins or bobbins attached to the project at once. By doing so, you're able to pick up each color as it's needed and then drop it (without cutting) when it's time to switch colors.

When dropping a color, make sure to drop it to the wrong side of the project so as to keep the right side free from any small yarn carries. It can be helpful to place a safety pin or stitch marker on the right side of a project after you've worked a few rows. This way you can easily tell which side to drop the strand of yarn when switching to a different color.

Sometimes you'll find that the color you need is already attached nearby, but not exactly right next to the tile you need to work. As you can see in the example below, it's possible to gently bring the red yarn over to the right (left for left-handed crocheters) in order to switch colors without cutting and reattaching the yarn. After completing the final yarn over of the last stitch with the red yarn, you can work the first red tile over the carried strand of yarn, thereby hiding it. Monitor the tension of the carried yarn carefully so that it doesn't cause the design to bunch up.

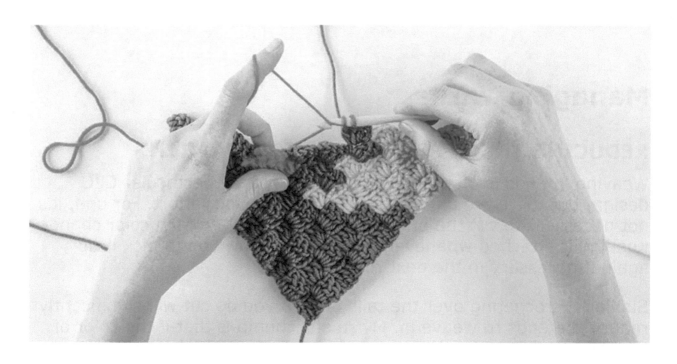

TIPS FOR WRANGLING YOUR YARN

As soon as you get the hang of switching colors with C2C crochet, your next question will likely be "How the heck do I keep all this yarn under control while I work?"!

You'll certainly figure out your own personal strategies for working with multiple balls of yarn at once, but here are some basic concepts to keep in mind:

Wind small bobbins

Find a tool that you like for creating small bobbins of yarn (read on for ideas) and then attach the bobbins to something that won't allow them to roll all over the place. For example, if you wind bobbins onto clothespins or industrial clips, clip them onto a basket in the order you'll need them in the pattern.

Be mindful of the direction you're flipping your work

Think of turning your work over like you're re-reading the same pages of a book. If you turn the "page" from left to right at the end of one row, be sure to turn it back from right to left on the next row. This will prevent your strands of working yarn from twisting together after a few rows.

Reduce rolling

If you're just working with a couple of skeins of yarn instead of many bobbins, it can still be very helpful to contain them in a way that prevents them from rolling around. Place the skeins in a box or basket and begin each skein from the middle rather than the outside so that the yarn doesn't need to roll each time you pull on the working strand (empty tissue boxes make great individual skein wranglers!).

Untangle as you go

It's bound to happen–you'll get all tangled up in the yarn and start to feel like a fly trapped in a spider web. Don't despair! Take a couple of moments to straighten out your yarn every few rows or at the end of a session of crocheting. Worst case, you can always cut the yarn and reattach it to your project.

TIP

Before starting a project, work one tile in a color, then unravel it and measure how much yarn the tile used. Look ahead in the graph and estimate how many tiles in that color you'll work with that bobbin. Then wind that approximate amount of yarn onto the bobbin.

TOOLS THAT CAN HELP

Small Bobbin Implements: Try winding bobbins on small household objects that you can attach to a stable basket, book, clothes hanger or even to the project itself. Some items that can work well include: clothespins, clips (binder clips, industrial clips, chip clips) or toilet paper tubes.

Containers With Holes: Use a simple household container, like a laundry basket, to place your skeins in. Pulling yarn from middle of skein, thread each color through a hole in the basket before you begin working with it. This method has the added advantage of giving you somewhere to easily contain your work-in-progress project in one place until you can pick it up again.

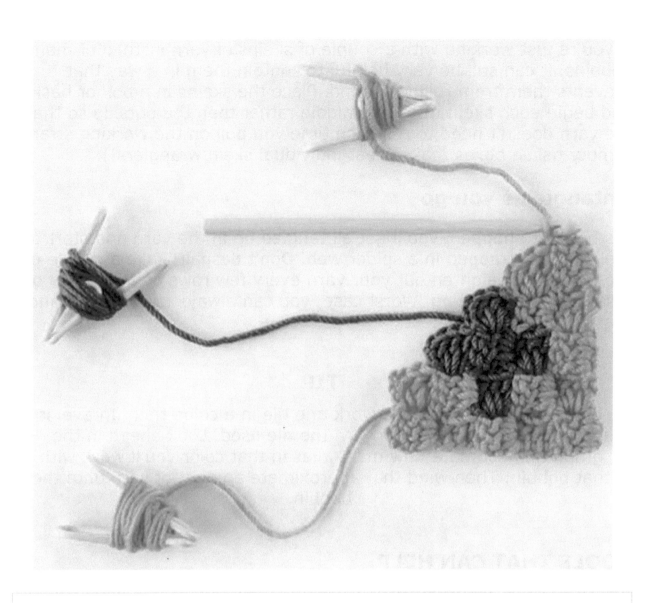

Bobbin Holders

Try a baby bottle drying rack or check Etsyfor C2C bobbin holders similar to the one pictured here. There are many talented woodworkers who have come up withfantastic solutions for crocheters like us. 1DogWoof.com even has a tutorial on how to make your modular bobbin holder.

HOW TO WEAVE IN ENDS

Some crocheters choose to weave in ends every few rows, while others may do them at the end of each day. Others still save them all for one glorious weaving session at the conclusion of a project.

In any case, weaving in the ends is also an opportunity to clean up any areas of your project where you'd like the individual tiles to be more visually connected. To do this, simply use a yarn tail to do a few whip stitches where you want the tiles to appear less separate. Then proceed with weaving in the end as described below. Weaving is usually done with a tapestry or upholstery needle, but a small crochet hook can also be used for dense projects.

Step 1: Thread yarn tail onto tapestry needle. Insert needle through the bottom "meatiest" section of a tile.

Step 2: Pass needle back through tile in opposite direction, taking care to pick up one vertical strand of yarn from the tile you're working through.

Step 3: Repeat Step 2.

3

Step 4: Snip yarn tail and celebrate being one step closer to a finished C2C project!

4

Repeat Steps 1-4 with each tail.

Projects

MIDTOWN STROLL
BABY BLANKET

A modern alternative to the classic crochet baby blanket, this gender-neutral blanket is perfect for city and country folk alike. Babies will love the graphic, high contrast patterns, while parents will appreciate a statement piece of handmade art for the nursery. Substitute the pale blue sky in favor of a brighter color for a Pop Art look. For an adult-sized throw, use a bulkier yarn and larger hook.

Difficulty Rating

Yarn

Lion Brand Vanna's Choice (100% acrylic), 4 worsted (10-ply/aran), 100g (70yd/156m), in the following shades:

› Silver Grey (149); 1 skein

› Dark Grey Heather (404); 1 skein

› Charcoal Grey (151); 2 skeins

› White (100); 1 skein

› Silver Blue (105); 3 skeins

Supplies

Size H (5mm) hook

Finished Size

$30^{1}/_{2}$ x $35^{1}/_{2}$in (77.5 x 90cm)

Gauge (Tension)

4 tiles measure $3^{1}/_{2}$in (9cm) using size H (5mm) hook and Lion Brand Vanna's Choice

Stitch

Double crochet (UK treble crochet) C2C

Instructions

TO MAKE THE BLANKET

› Follow the written pattern and graph to crochet the blanket.

› Weave in all ends (I promise, you can do it!).

› For the border, work one round of single crochet border (see General Techniques: Single Crochet Border), followed by one round of crab stitch border (see General Techniques: Crab Stitch Border). For each border, use Silver Blue around the 'sky' section and Charcoal Grey around the 'city' section.

TIP

This project requires a fairly high number of color changes. To minimize the number of times you need to cut the yarn, create multiple working bobbins of the same color.

Pattern

◄ **Row 1 [RS]:** Charcoal x 1

► **Row 2 [WS]:** Charcoal x 2

◄ **Row 3:** Charcoal x 2, Heather x 1

► **Row 4:** Heather x 2, Charcoal x 2

◄ **Row 5:** Charcoal x 2, Heather x 3

► **Row 6:** Heather x 2, White x 1, Heather x 1, Charcoal x 2

◄ **Row 7:** Charcoal x 2, Heather x 5

► **Row 8:** Heather x 2, (White x 1, Heather x 1) twice, Charcoal x 2

◄ **Row 9:** Charcoal x 2, Heather x 7

► **Row 10:** Silver x 1, (Heather x 1, White x 1) 3 times, Heather x 1, Charcoal x 2

◄ **Row 11:** Charcoal x 2, Heather x 7, Silver x 1, Charcoal x 1

► **Row 12:** Charcoal x 2, Silver x 1, Heather x 1, (White x 1, Heather x 1) 3 times, Charcoal x 2

◄ **Row 13:** Charcoal x 2, Heather x 7, Silver x 1, Charcoal x 3

► **Row 14:** Heather x 1, Charcoal x 3, Silver x 1, (Heather x 1, White x 1) 3 times, Heather x 1, Charcoal x 2

◄ **Row 15:** Charcoal x 2, Heather x 7, Silver x 1, Charcoal x 3, Heather x 2

► **Row 16:** Heather x 3, Charcoal x 3, Silver x 1, (Heather x 1, White x 1) twice, Heather x 3, Charcoal x 2

◄ **Row 17:** Charcoal x 3, Heather x 6, Silver x 1, Charcoal x 3, Heather x 1, White x 1, Heather x 2

► **Row 18:** Heather x 2, White x 1, Heather x 2, Charcoal x 3, Silver x 1, Heather x 1, White x 1, Heather x 3, Charcoal x 3, Blue x 1

◄ **Row 19:** Blue x 2, Charcoal x 2, Silver x 2, Heather x 3, Silver x 1, Charcoal x 3, (Heather x 1, White x 1) twice, Heather x 1, Charcoal x 1

► **Row 20:** Charcoal x 2, Heather x 2, White x 1, Heather x 2, Charcoal x 3, Silver x 1, Heather x 1, Silver x 1, White x 1, Silver x 2, Charcoal x 1, Blue x 3

◄ **Row 21:** Blue x 4, Silver x 2, (White x 1, Silver x 1) twice, Charcoal x 3, (Heather x 1, White x 1) twice, Heather x 1, Charcoal x 2, Silver x 1

▶ **Row 22:** Silver x 2, Charcoal x 2, Heather x 2, White x 1, Heather x 2, Charcoal x 3, (Silver x 1, White x 1) twice, Silver x 2, Blue x 4

◀ **Row 23:** Blue x 4, Silver x 2, (White x 1, Silver x 1) twice, Charcoal x 3, (Heather x 1, White x 1) twice, Heather x 1, Charcoal x 2, Silver x 3

▶ **Row 24:** Charcoal x 1, Silver x 3, Charcoal x 2, Heather x 2, White x 1, Heather x 1, Charcoal x 4, (Silver x 1, White x 1) twice, Silver x 2, Blue x 4

◀ **Row 25:** Blue x 5, (Silver x 1, White x 1) twice, Silver x 1, Charcoal x 5, Heather x 1, White x 1, Heather x 1, Charcoal x 2, Silver x 3, Charcoal x 2

▶ **Row 26:** Charcoal x 3, Silver x 3, Charcoal x 2, Heather x 2, Blue x 1, Charcoal x 5, (Silver x 1, White x 1) twice, Silver x 1, Blue x 5

◀ **Row 27:** Blue x 5, (Silver x 1, White x 1) twice, Silver x 1, Charcoal x 5, Blue x 2, Heather x 1, Charcoal x 2, Silver x 3, Charcoal x 1, White x 1, Charcoal x 2

▶ **Row 28:** Heather x 1, Charcoal x 4, Silver x 3, Charcoal x 3, Blue x 2, Charcoal x 5, (Silver x 1, White x 1) twice, Silver x 1, Blue x 5

◀ **Row 29:** Blue x 6, Silver x 2, White x 1, Silver x 1, White x 1, Silver x 2, Blue x 4, Charcoal x 3, Silver x 3, Charcoal x 3, White x 1, Heather x 2

▶ **Row 30:** Heather x 3, Charcoal x 2, White x 1, Charcoal x 1, Silver x 3, Charcoal x 3, Blue x 4, Silver x 2, White x 1, Silver x 1, White x 1, Silver x 2, Blue x 6

◀ **Row 31:** Blue x 6, Silver x 4, White x 1, Silver x 2, Blue x 4, Silver x 1, Charcoal x 2, Silver x 3, Charcoal x 4, Heather x 3, Silver x 1

▶ **Row 32:** Heather x 1, White x 1, Heather x 3, White x 1, Charcoal x 3, Silver x 3, Charcoal x 1, Silver x 2, Blue x 4, Silver x 2, White x 1, Silver x 3, Blue x 7

◀ **Row 33:** Blue x 8, Silver x 4, Blue x 5, Silver x 6, Charcoal x 1, White x 1, Charcoal x 2, Heather x 3, Silver x 1, Heather x 2

▶ **Row 34:** Heather x 3, Silver x 1, Heather x 3, Charcoal x 4, Silver x 6, Blue x 5, Silver x 4, Blue x 8

◀ **Row 35:** Blue x 8, Silver x 1, Blue x 1, Silver x 1, Blue x 6, Silver x 6, Charcoal x 3, White x 1, Heather x 3, White x 1, Heather x 1, White x 1, Heather x 2

CORNER *(decrease at beginning of WS rows, increase at beginning of RS rows)*

▶ **Row 36 [WS]:** Heather x 1, White x 2, Heather x 1, Silver x 1, Heather x 2, Charcoal x 3, White x 1, Charcoal x 1, Silver x 5, Blue x 9, Silver x 1, Blue x 8

◀ **Row 37 [RS]:** Blue x 8, Silver x 1, Blue x 10, Silver x 4, Charcoal x 5, Heather x 2, Silver x 1, Heather x 2, White x 1, Heather x 1

▶ **Row 38:** Heather x 4, White x 1, Silver x 2, Charcoal x 1, White x 1, Charcoal x 2, Blue x 1, Silver x 3, Blue x 20

◀ **Row 39:** Blue x 21, Silver x 2, Blue x 1, Charcoal x 4, White x 1, Silver x 2, Heather x 1, White x 1, Heather x 2

CORNER *(decrease at beginning of each row)*

▶ **Row 40 [WS]:** Heather x 1, White x 2, Heather x 1, Silver x 1, White x 1, Silver x 1, Charcoal x 4, Blue x 1, Silver x 1, Blue x 21

◀ **Row 41 [RS]:** Blue x 22, Charcoal x 4, Silver x 2, White x 1, Heather x 2, White x 1, Heather x 1

▶ **Row 42:** Heather x 3, Silver x 3, White x 1, Silver x 1, Charcoal x 2, Blue x 22

◀ **Row 43:** Blue x 21, Charcoal x 2, Silver x 2, White x 1, Silver x 2, Blue x 1, Heather x 2

▶ **Row 44:** Heather x 1, Blue x 2, Silver x 1, White x 1, Silver x 2, White x 1, Silver x 1, Charcoal x 1, Blue x 20

◀ **Row 45:** Blue x 19, Charcoal x 1, Silver x 2, White x 1, Silver x 3, Blue x 3

▶ **Row 46:** Blue x 3, (Silver x 2, White x 1) twice, Silver x 1, Blue x 18

◀ **Row 47:** Blue x 18, Silver x 1, White x 1, Silver x 2, White x 1, Silver x 1, Blue x 3

▶ **Row 48:** Blue x 3, Silver x 3, White x 1, Silver x 2, Blue x 17

◀ **Row 49:** Blue x 17, Silver x 2, White x 1, Silver x 2, Blue x 3

▶ **Row 50:** Blue x 3, Silver x 1, White x 1, Silver x 3, Blue x 16

◀ **Row 51:** Blue x 16, Silver x 4, Blue x 3

▶ **Row 52:** Blue x 3, Silver x 4, Blue x 15

◄ **Row 53:** Blue x 15, Silver x 3, Blue x 3

▶ **Row 54:** Blue x 3, Silver x 3, Blue x 14

◄ **Row 55:** Blue x 14, Silver x 2, Blue x 3

▶ **Row 56:** Blue x 3, Silver x 2, Blue x 13

◄ **Row 57:** Blue x 13, Silver x 1, Blue x 3

▶ **Row 58:** Blue x 3, Silver x 1, Blue x 12

◄ **Row 59:** Blue x 15

▶ **Row 60:** Blue x 14

◄ **Row 61:** Blue x 13

▶ **Row 62:** Blue x 12

◄ **Row 63:** Blue x 11

▶ **Row 64:** Blue x 10

◄ **Row 65:** Blue x 9

▶ **Row 66:** Blue x 8

◄ **Row 67:** Blue x 7

▶ **Row 68:** Blue x 6

◄ **Row 69:** Blue x 5

▶ **Row 70:** Blue x 4

◄ **Row 71:** Blue x 3

▶ **Row 72:** Blue x 2

◄ **Row 73:** Blue x 1

MIDTOWN STROLL BABY BLANKET GRAPH

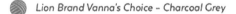 Lion Brand Vanna's Choice – Charcoal Grey

Lion Brand Vanna's Choice – Dark Grey Heather

Lion Brand Vanna's Choice – White

Lion Brand Vanna's Choice – Silver Grey

Lion Brand Vanna's Choice – Silver Blue

FADED ARROWS
THROW

Make your own catalogue-worthy throw with this relatively easy graphgan. Once you've mastered the basic C2C stitch, this is an excellent project to practice color changes while making something really beautiful in the process. The jersey-like quality of this yarn creates precise stitch definition while the low contrast pattern is sophisticated enough for any room in the house.

Difficulty Rating

Yarn

Bernat Maker Home Dec (72% cotton, 28% nylon), 5 bulky (12/14-ply/chunky), 250g (317yd/290m), in the following shades:

> Clay (11008); 7 skeins

> Cream (11009); 2 skeins

Supplies

Size K (6.5mm) hook

Smaller hook for weaving in ends

Tassel maker or $5^3/_4$in (14.5cm) piece of cardboard

Finished Size

$41^1/_2$ x 50in (105.5 x 19.5cm) excluding tassels

Gauge (Tension)

4 tiles measure $3^1/_2$in (9cm) using size K (6.5mm) hook and Bernat Maker Home Dec

Stitch

Double crochet (UK treble crochet) C2C

NOTES

◢ *The style of this blanket will vary greatly based on fiber and colors used. Don't be afraid to experiment!*

◢ *Similarly, swap out the tassels for a border of fluffy pom poms around the two shorter blanket sides for a more playful look.*

Instructions

TO MAKE THE THROW

› Follow the written pattern and graph to crochet the throw.

› For the border, using Clay, work one round of single crochet border (see General Techniques: Single Crochet Border). Fasten off.

› To finish, weave in all ends.

› Using a tassel maker set to $5^3/_4$in (14cm) or a $5^3/_4$in (14cm) piece of cardboard and last skein of Cream, make 8 chunky tassels. Wrap yarn approximately 75 times to get the tassel density pictured. Use a tapestry needle to attach two tassels to each corner of blanket (see General Techniques: Making a Tassel).

TIP

Because of the fabric-like structure of this yarn, you may find it easier to use a smaller hook instead of a tapestry needle to weave in ends.

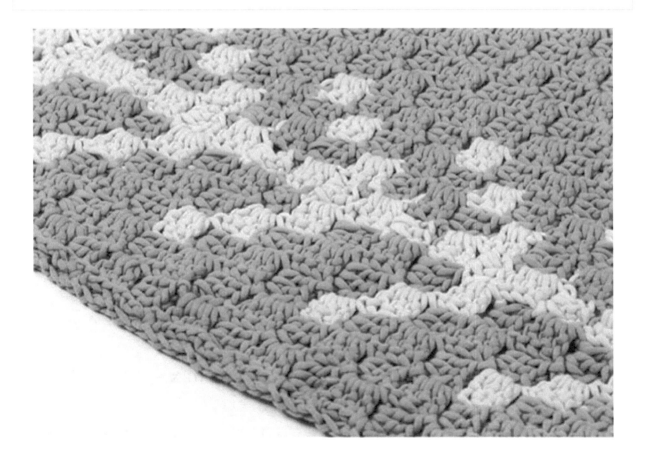

Pattern

◀ **Row 1 [RS]:** Clay x 1

▶ **Row 2 [WS]:** Clay x 2

◀ **Row 3:** Clay x 3

▶ **Row 4:** Clay x 4

◀ **Row 5:** Clay x 5

▶ **Row 6:** Clay x 2, Cream x 4

◀ **Row 7:** Clay x 1, Cream x 1, Clay x 5

▶ **Row 8:** Clay x 5, Cream x 2, Clay x 1

◀ **Row 9:** Clay x 3, Cream x 4, Clay x 2

▶ **Row 10:** Clay x 5, Cream x 1, Clay x 1, Cream x 1, Clay x 2

◀ **Row 11:** Clay x 4, Cream x 2, Clay x 5

▶ **Row 12:** Clay x 5, Cream x 1, Clay x 2, Cream x 1, Clay x 3

◀ **Row 13:** Clay x 5, Cream x 1, Clay x 1, Cream x 4, Clay x 2

▶ **Row 14:** Clay x 5, Cream x 1, Clay x 8

◀ **Row 15:** Clay x 6, Cream x 1, Clay x 1, Cream x 2, Clay x 5

▶ **Row 16:** Clay x 5, Cream x 1, Clay x 10

◀ **Row 17:** Clay x 9, Cream x 1, Clay x 1, Cream x 4, Clay x 2

▶ **Row 18:** Clay x 5, Cream x 1, Clay x 12

◀ **Row 19:** Clay x 10, Cream x 1, Clay x 1, Cream x 2, Clay x 5

▶ **Row 20:** Clay x 5, Cream x 1, Clay x 14

◀ **Row 21:** Clay x 13, Cream x 1, Clay x 1, Cream x 4, Clay x 2

▶ **Row 22:** Clay x 5, Cream x 1, Clay x 16

◀ **Row 23:** Clay x 14, Cream x 1, Clay x 1, Cream x 2, Clay x 5

▶ **Row 24:** Clay x 5, Cream x 1, Clay x 18

◀ **Row 25:** Clay x 17, Cream x 1, Clay x 1, Cream x 4, Clay x 2

▶ **Row 26:** Clay x 5, Cream x 1, Clay x 20

◀ **Row 27:** Clay x 18, Cream x 1, Clay x 1, Cream x 2, Clay x 5

▶ **Row 28:** Clay x 5, Cream x 1, Clay x 22

◀ **Row 29:** Clay x 21, Cream x 1, Clay x 1, Cream x 4, Clay x 2

▶ **Row 30:** Clay x 5, Cream x 1, Clay x 24

◀ **Row 31:** Clay x 22, Cream x 1, Clay x 1, Cream x 2, Clay x 5

▶ **Row 32:** Clay x 5, Cream x 1, Clay x 26

◀ **Row 33:** Clay x 25, Cream x 1, Clay x 1, Cream x 4, Clay x 2

▶ **Row 34:** Clay x 5, Cream x 1, Clay x 28

◀ **Row 35:** Clay x 26, Cream x 1, Clay x 1, Cream x 2, Clay x 5

▶ **Row 36:** Clay x 5, Cream x 1, Clay x 30

◀ **Row 37:** Clay x 29, Cream x 1, Clay x 1, Cream x 4, Clay x 2

▶ **Row 38:** Clay x 5, Cream x 1, Clay x 32

◀ **Row 39:** Clay x 30, Cream x 1, Clay x 1, Cream x 2, Clay x 5

▶ **Row 40:** Clay x 5, Cream x 1, Clay x 34

◀ **Row 41:** Clay x 33, Cream x 1, Clay x 1, Cream x 4, Clay x 2

▶ **Row 42:** Clay x 5, Cream x 1, Clay x 36

◀ **Row 43:** Clay x 34, Cream x 1, Clay x 1, Cream x 2, Clay x 5

▶ **Row 44:** Clay x 5, Cream x 1, Clay x 38

◀ **Row 45:** Clay x 37, Cream x 1, Clay x 1, Cream x 4, Clay x 2

▶ **Row 46:** Clay x 5, Cream x 1, Clay x 40

◀ **Row 47:** Clay x 38, Cream x 1, Clay x 1, Cream x 2, Clay x 5

CORNER *(increase at beginning of all RS rows, decrease at beginning of all WS rows)*

▶ **Row 48 [WS]:** Clay x 4, Cream x 1, Clay x 42

◀ **Row 49 [RS]:** Clay x 41, Cream x 1, Clay x 1, Cream x 4

▶ **Row 50:** Clay x 2, Cream x 1, Clay x 42, Cream x 1, Clay x 1

◀ **Row 51:** Clay x 42, Cream x 1, Clay x 1, Cream x 2, Clay x 1

▶ **Row 52:** Cream x 1, Clay x 43, Cream x 1, Clay x 1, Cream x 1

◀ **Row 53:** Clay x 1, Cream x 1, Clay x 2, Cream x 1, Clay x 40, Cream x 1, Clay x 1

▶ **Row 54:** Clay x 43, Cream x 2, Clay x 2

◄ **Row 55:** Clay x 3, Cream x 1, Clay x 1, Cream x 1, Clay x 40, Cream x 1

▶ **Row 56:** Clay x 42, Cream x 4, Clay x 1

◄ **Row 57:** Clay x 5, Cream x 2, Clay x 1, Cream x 1, Clay x 38

CORNER *(decrease at beginning of each row)*

▶ **Row 58 [WS]:** Clay x 40, Cream x 1, Clay x 5

◄ **Row 59 [RS]:** Clay x 2, Cream x 4, Clay x 1, Cream x 1, Clay x 37

▶ **Row 60:** Clay x 38, Cream x 1, Clay x 5

◄ **Row 61:** Clay x 5, Cream x 2, Clay x 1, Cream x 1, Clay x 34

▶ **Row 62:** Clay x 36, Cream x 1, Clay x 5

◄ **Row 63:** Clay x 2, Cream x 4, Clay x 1, Cream x 1, Clay x 33

▶ **Row 64:** Clay x 34, Cream x 1, Clay x 5

◄ **Row 65:** Clay x 5, Cream x 2, Clay x 1, Cream x 1, Clay x 30

▶ **Row 66:** Clay x 32, Cream x 1, Clay x 5

◄ **Row 67:** Clay x 2, Cream x 4, Clay x 1, Cream x 1, Clay x 29

▶ **Row 68:** Clay x 30, Cream x 1, Clay x 5

◄ **Row 69:** Clay x 5, Cream x 2, Clay x 1, Cream x 1, Clay x 26

▶ **Row 70:** Clay x 28, Cream x 1, Clay x 5

◄ **Row 71:** Clay x 2, Cream x 4, Clay x 1, Cream x 1, Clay x 25

▶ **Row 72:** Clay x 26, Cream x 1, Clay x 5

◄ **Row 73:** Clay x 5, Cream x 2, Clay x 1, Cream x 1, Clay x 22

▶ **Row 74:** Clay x 24, Cream x 1, Clay x 5

◄ **Row 75:** Clay x 2, Cream x 4, Clay x 1, Cream x 1, Clay x 21

▶ **Row 76:** Clay x 22, Cream x 1, Clay x 5

◄ **Row 77:** Clay x 5, Cream x 2, Clay x 1, Cream x 1, Clay x 18

▶ **Row 78:** Clay x 20, Cream x 1, Clay x 5

◄ **Row 79:** Clay x 2, Cream x 4, Clay x 1, Cream x 1, Clay x 17

▶ **Row 80:** Clay x 18, Cream x 1, Clay x 5

◄ **Row 81:** Clay x 5, Cream x 2, Clay x 1, Cream x 1, Clay x 14

▶ **Row 82:** Clay x 16, Cream x 1, Clay x 5

◀ **Row 83:** Clay x 2, Cream x 4, Clay x 1, Cream x 1, Clay x 13

▶ **Row 84:** Clay x 14, Cream x 1, Clay x 5

◀ **Row 85:** Clay x 5, Cream x 2, Clay x 1, Cream x 1, Clay x 10

▶ **Row 86:** Clay x 12, Cream x 1, Clay x 5

◀ **Row 87:** Clay x 2, Cream x 4, Clay x 1, Cream x 1, Clay x 9

▶ **Row 88:** Clay x 10, Cream x 1, Clay x 5

◀ **Row 89:** Clay x 5, Cream x 2, Clay x 1, Cream x 1, Clay x 6

▶ **Row 90:** Clay x 8, Cream x 1, Clay x 5

◀ **Row 91:** Clay x 2, Cream x 4, Clay x 1, Cream x 1, Clay x 5

▶ **Row 92:** Clay x 6, Cream x 1, Clay x 5

◀ **Row 93:** Clay x 5, Cream x 2, Clay x 1, Cream x 1, Clay x 2

▶ **Row 94:** Clay x 4, Cream x 1, Clay x 5

◀ **Row 95:** Clay x 2, Cream x 4, Clay x 1, Cream x 1, Clay x 1

▶ **Row 96:** Clay x 2, Cream x 1, Clay x 5

◀ **Row 97:** Clay x 5, Cream x 2

▶ **Row 98:** Cream x 1, Clay x 5

◀ **Row 99:** Clay x 2, Cream x 3

▶ **Row 100:** Clay x 4

◀ **Row 101:** Clay x 3

▶ **Row 102:** Clay x 2

◀ **Row 103:** Clay x 1

TIP

Try this pattern in worsted weight yarn with a smaller hook to make a baby-sized blanket.

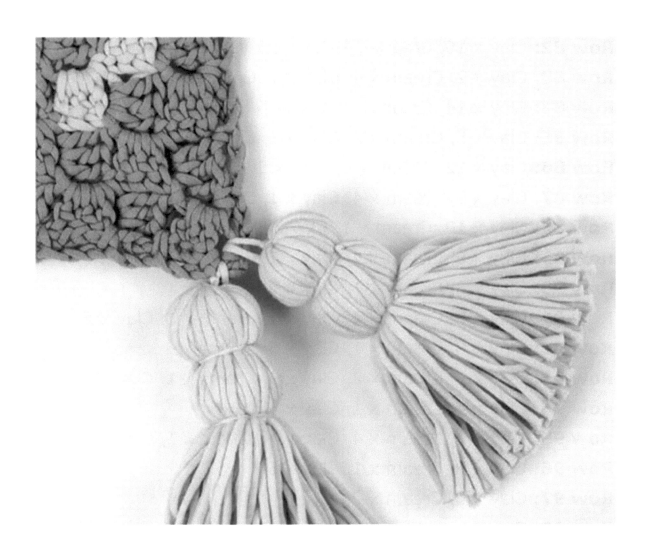

FADED ARROWS THROW GRAPH

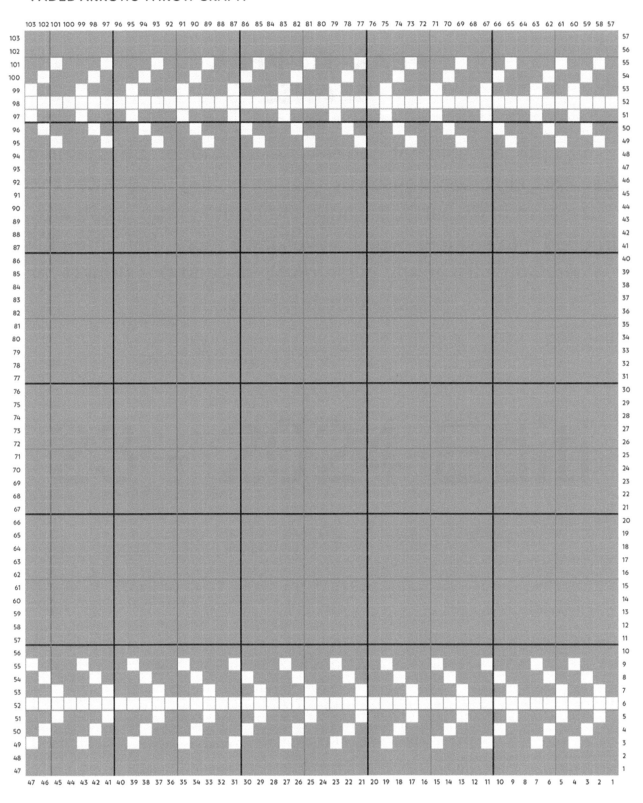

Bernat Maker Home Dec – Clay

Bernat Maker Home Dec – Cream

PEAK-TO-PEAK
BEANIE

This approachable hat pattern is proof that an unassuming C2C rectangle can transform into something far greater than the sum of its parts. Because the colors in the graph are grouped into sections, you'll never have more than three balls of working yarn at any given point, making this project far easier than it looks.

Difficulty Rating

Yarn

Wool and The Gang Feeling Good Yarn (70% alpaca, 23% nylon, 7% merino), 4 worsted (10-ply/aran), 50g (142yd/130m), in the following shades:

> Cameo Rose; 1 skein

> Forest Green; 1 skein

> Mellow Mauve; 1 skein

Supplies

Size K (6.5mm) hook

Fur pom pom, size $4^{1}/_{2}$in (11.5cm)

Measurements and Sizing

One size: to fit average woman's head

Circumference: approx. $19^{1}/_{2}$in (49.5cm)

Height: $9^{3}/_{4}$in (24.75cm) with brim folded up, excluding pom pom

Gauge (Tension)

4 tiles measure $3^{1}/_{4}$in (8.25cm) using size K (6.5mm) hook and Wool and The Gang Feeling Good Yarn

Stitch

Double crochet (UK treble crochet) C2C

NOTES

◢ *Since each section of color is continuous, work this graph without cutting yarn at color changes. Instead, simply drop first color to the WS and pick up second color. Then the old color will be conveniently waiting there to be picked up on the next row.*

Instructions

TO MAKE THE BEANIE HAT

› Follow the written pattern and graph to crochet the main hat rectangle. Fasten off leaving a 12in (30cm) tail on each color.

› For the ribbing, using Forest Green, work ribbing as written below. Slip stitches can have a tendency to get quite tight, so take care to work them fairly loosely if you're having trouble inserting your hook.

Ribbing Foundation Row: Ch 12.

Row 1: Sk first ch, slst in each ch to end of row; turn. (11)

Rows 2-84: Ch 1, sc in the back loop of each slst; turn.

Piece should have 42 bumps of ribbing. Fasten off leaving a 30in (76cm) tail.

› For joining, pieces technically have no RS or WS, so choose the best-looking sides and designate the RS.

› Complete all seaming with a tapestry needle and the stitch described in Joining C2C Pieces (see General Techniques).

› With WS facing up, place ribbing along bottom edge of hat piece. Using the leftover strand of Forest Green, sew ribbing to hat (see General Techniques: Joining C2C Pieces).

› Fold hat rectangle width-wise so that two shortest sides are touching and WS is facing out. With tapestry needle and tails left over from working rectangle, seam each section of color and ribbing (see General Techniques: Joining C2C Pieces).

› With one strand of Cameo Rose and tapestry needle, close top of hat by whip stitching around top edge of rectangle. Pull gently to gather rectangle. It's okay if there is a small hole at the top of the hat as the pom pom will cover it.

› Turn hat RS out. With same strand of yarn, sew pom pom to top of hat. Fasten off.

› Weave in any remaining ends. Fold ribbed brim of hat up as pictured.

Pattern

◀ **Row 1 [RS]:** Green x 1

▶ **Row 2 [WS]:** Green x 2

◀ **Row 3:** Green x 3

▶ **Row 4:** Green x 4

◀ **Row 5:** Green x 5

▶ **Row 6:** Green x 5, Mauve x 1

◀ **Row 7:** Mauve x 1, Green x 6

▶ **Row 8:** Green x 4, Mauve x 4

◀ **Row 9:** Mauve x 4, Green x 5

▶ **Row 10:** Green x 5, Mauve x 3, Rose x 2

◀ **Row 11:** Rose x 2, Mauve x 3, Green x 6

▶ **Row 12:** Green x 4, Mauve x 5, Rose x 3

◀ **Row 13:** Rose x 3, Mauve x 5, Green x 5

CORNER *(increase at beginning of WS rows, decrease at beginning of RS rows)*

▶ **Row 14 [WS]:** Green x 5, Mauve x 3, Rose x 5

◀ **Row 15 [RS]:** Rose x 4, Mauve x 3, Green x 6

▶ **Row 16:** Green x 4, Mauve x 5, Rose x 4

◀ **Row 17:** Rose x 3, Mauve x 5, Green x 5

▶ **Row 18:** Green x 5, Mauve x 3, Rose x 5

◀ **Row 19:** Rose x 4, Mauve x 3, Green x 6

▶ **Row 20:** Green x 4, Mauve x 5, Rose x 4

◀ **Row 21:** Rose x 3, Mauve x 5, Green x 5

▶ **Row 22:** Green x 5, Mauve x 3, Rose x 5

◀ **Row 23:** Rose x 4, Mauve x 3, Green x 6

▶ **Row 24:** Green x 4, Mauve x 5, Rose x 4

CORNER *(decrease at beginning of each row)*

◀ **Row 25 [RS]:** Rose x 3, Mauve x 5, Green x 4

▶ **Row 26 [WS]:** Green x 3, Mauve x 3, Rose x 5

◀ **Row 27:** Rose x 4, Mauve x 3, Green x 3

▶ **Row 28:** Mauve x 5, Rose x 4

◀ **Row 29:** Rose x 3, Mauve x 5

▶ **Row 30:** Mauve x 2, Rose x 5

◀ **Row 31:** Rose x 4, Mauve x 2

▶ **Row 32:** Mauve x 1, Rose x 4

◀ **Row 33:** Rose x 3, Mauve x 1

▶ **Row 34:** Rose x 3

◀ **Row 35:** Rose x 2

▶ **Row 36 :** Rose x 1

PEAK-TO-PEAK BEANIE GRAPH

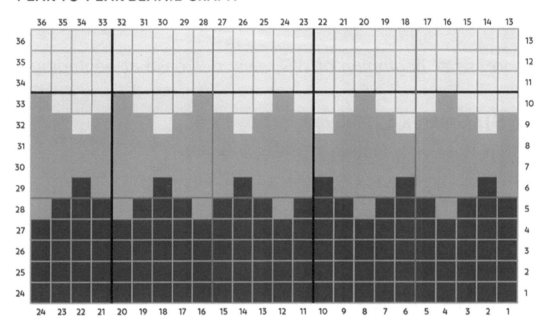

Wool and The Gang Feeling Good Yarn – Cameo Rose

Wool and The Gang Feeling Good Yarn – Mellow Mauve

Wool and The Gang Feeling Good Yarn – Forest Green

WEE WANDERER
BABY BLANKET

Keep your little explorers warm on their adventures with this modern child-sized blanket. While the design may look complicated, it requires relatively little bobbin management because the colors are worked in sections. Crochet it as pictured, or practice your color theory skills by swapping out shades for different overlapping combinations.

Difficulty Rating

Yarn

Caron Simply Soft (100% acrylic), 4 worsted (10-ply/aran), 170g (314yd/288m), in the following shades:

› Off White (9702); 4 skeins
› Plum Perfect (9761); 1 skein
› Kelly Green (9769); 1 skein
› Persimmon (9754); 1 skein
› Chartreuse (9771); 1 skein
› Ocean (9759); 1 skein
› Robin's Egg Blue (9780); 1 skein
› Lavender Blue (9756); 1 skein
› Gold (9782); 1 skein
› Sunshine (9755); 1 skein

Supplies

Size H (5mm) hook

Finished Size

$36^1/_2$ x $36^1/_2$in (93 x 93cm)

Gauge (Tension)

4 tiles measure $2^3/_4$in (7cm) using size H (5mm) hook and Caron Simply Soft

Stitch

Double crochet (UK treble crochet) C2C

NOTES

◢ *This is a fun blanket to experiment with adding a more decorative border if desired. Simply work a basic single crochet border (see General Techniques: Single Crochet Border) to create a foundation round and then add your favorite "fancy" border in the next round(s).*

◢ *Since each color is used in a large section, do not cut yarn at color changes. Instead keep first color attached when switching to second color (see Changing Color). Then when working back in the opposite direction with second color, pick up first color when appropriate.*

Instructions

TO MAKE THE BLANKET

› Follow the written pattern and graph to crochet the blanket.

› For the border, work 3 rounds as follows:

Border Round 1: Attach Ocean and work one round of single crochet border (see General Techniques: Single Crochet Border).

Border Round 2: Continue with Ocean, ch 2 (does not count as a st), hdc in first sc, *2 hdc in next ch2sp, hdc in next sc; repeat from * to beginning of round working 2 hdc in both sc sts at each corner, slst to second ch from beginning of round to join. Fasten off.

Border Round 3: Attach Plum Perfect, work one round of crab stitch border (see General Techniques: Crab Stitch Border). Fasten off.

Weave in any remaining ends.

Pattern

◀ **Row 1 [RS]:** Off White x 1

▶ **Row 2 [WS]:** Off White x 2

◀ **Row 3:** Off White x 3

▶ **Row 4:** Off White x 4

◀ **Row 5:** Off White x 5

▶ **Row 6:** Off White x 6

◀ **Row 7:** Off White x 7

▶ **Row 8:** Off White x 8

◀ **Row 9:** Off White x 9

▶ **Row 10:** Off White x 10

◀ **Row 11:** Off White x 11

▶ **Row 12:** Off White x 12

◀ **Row 13:** Off White x 13

▶ **Row 14:** Off White x 14

◀ **Row 15:** Off White x 15

▶ **Row 16:** Off White x 16

◀ **Row 17:** Off White x 17

▶ **Row 18:** Off White x 18

◀ **Row 19:** Off White x 19

▶ **Row 20:** Off White x 20

◀ **Row 21:** Off White x 6, Chartreuse x 1, Off White x 14

▶ **Row 22:** Off White x 14, Chartreuse x 2, Off White x 6

◀ **Row 23:** Off White x 6, Chartreuse x 3, Off White x 14

▶ **Row 24:** Off White x 14, Chartreuse x 4, Off White x 6

◀ **Row 25:** Off White x 7, Chartreuse x 4, Off White x 14

▶ **Row 26:** Off White x 14, Chartreuse x 5, Off White x 7

◀ **Row 27:** Off White x 7, Chartreuse x 5, Green x 1, Off White x 14

▶ **Row 28:** Off White x 14, Green x 2, Chartreuse x 5, Off White x 7

◀ **Row 29:** Off White x 8, Chartreuse x 5, Green x 2, Off White x 14

▶ **Row 30:** Off White x 14, Green x 3, Chartreuse x 5, Off White x 8

◀ **Row 31:** Off White x 8, Chartreuse x 5, Green x 4, Off White x 14

▶ **Row 32:** Off White x 14, Green x 4, Chartreuse x 6, Off White x 8

◀ **Row 33:** Off White x 9, Chartreuse x 5, Green x 5, Off White x 14

▶ **Row 34:** Off White x 14, Plum x 1, Green x 5, Chartreuse x 5, Off White x 9

◀ **Row 35:** Off White x 9, Chartreuse x 6, Green x 5, Plum x 1, Off White x 14

▶ **Row 36:** Off White x 14, Plum x 2, Green x 5, Chartreuse x 6, Off White x 9

◀ **Row 37:** Off White x 10, Chartreuse x 5, Green x 6, Plum x 2, Off White x 14

▶ **Row 38:** Off White x 14, Plum x 3, Green x 5, Chartreuse x 6, Off White x 10

◀ **Row 39:** Off White x 10, Chartreuse x 6, Green x 6, Plum x 3, Off White x 14

▶ **Row 40:** Off White x 14, Plum x 4, Green x 6, Chartreuse x 6, Off White x 10

◀ **Row 41:** Off White x 10, Chartreuse x 7, Green x 6, Plum x 4, Off White x 14

▶ **Row 42:** Off White x 14, Ocean x 5, Blue x 6, Off White x 17

◀ **Row 43:** Off White x 17, Blue x 7, Ocean x 5, Off White x 14

▶ **Row 44:** Off White x 14, Ocean x 6, Blue x 6, Off White x 18

◀ **Row 45:** Off White x 18, Blue x 7, Ocean x 6, Off White x 14

▶ **Row 46:** Off White x 14, Lavender x 1, Ocean x 6, Blue x 7, Off White x 18

◀ **Row 47:** Off White x 19, Blue x 7, Ocean x 5, Lavender x 2, Off White x 14

▶ **Row 48:** Off White x 14, Lavender x 4, Ocean x 4, Blue x 7, Off White x 19

◀ **Row 49:** Off White x 10, Persimmon x 3, Off White x 6, Blue x 8, Ocean x 3, Lavender x 5, Off White x 14

▶ **Row 50:** Off White x 14, Lavender x 7, Ocean x 2, Blue x 7, Off White x 6, Persimmon x 3, Gold x 1, Off White x 10

◀ **Row 51:** Off White x 10, Gold x 2, Persimmon x 3, Off White x 5, Blue x 8, Ocean x 1, Lavender x 8, Off White x 14

▶ **Row 52:** Off White x 14, Lavender x 9, Ocean x 1, Blue x 8, Off White x 4, Persimmon x 3, Gold x 3, Off White x 10

CORNER *(decrease at beginning of each row)*

◀ **Row 53 [RS]:** Off White x 10, Gold x 3, Persimmon x 2, Off White x 5, Blue x 7, Off White x 1, Lavender x 10, Off White x 13

▶ **Row 54 [WS]:** Off White x 12, Lavender x 11, Off White x 2, Blue x 6, Off White x 4, Persimmon x 2, Gold x 3, Sunshine x 1, Off White x 9

◀ **Row 55:** Off White x 9, Sunshine x 1, Gold x 3, Persimmon x 1, Off White x 4, Blue x 6, Off White x 3, Lavender x 11, Off White x 11

▶ **Row 56:** Off White x 10, Lavender x 12, Off White x 4, Blue x 4, Off White x 4, Persimmon x 1, Gold x 3, Sunshine x 2, Off White x 8

◀ **Row 57:** Off White x 8, Sunshine x 2, Gold x 3, Off White x 4, Blue x 4, Off White x 5, Lavender x 12, Off White x 9

▶ **Row 58:** Off White x 8, Lavender x 13, Off White x 6, Blue x 3, Off White x 4, Gold x 2, Sunshine x 2, Off White x 8

◀ **Row 59:** Off White x 8, Sunshine x 2, Gold x 1, Off White x 5, Blue x 2, Off White x 7, Lavender x 13, Off White x 7

▶ **Row 60:** Off White x 7, Lavender x 13, Off White x 8, Blue x 1, Off White x 15

◀ **Row 61:** Off White x 14, Blue x 1, Off White x 9, Lavender x 12, Off White x 7

▶ **Row 62:** Off White x 8, Lavender x 11, Off White x 23

◀ **Row 63:** Off White x 23, Lavender x 10, Off White x 8

▶ **Row 64:** Off White x 9, Lavender x 9, Off White x 22

◀ **Row 65:** Off White x 22, Lavender x 8, Off White x 9

▶ **Row 66:** Off White x 10, Lavender x 7, Off White x 21

◀ **Row 67:** Off White x 21, Lavender x 6, Off White x 10

▶ **Row 68:** Off White x 11, Lavender x 5, Off White x 20

◀ **Row 69:** Off White x 20, Lavender x 4, Off White x 11

▶ **Row 70:** Off White x 12, Lavender x 3, Off White x 19

◀ **Row 71:** Off White x 19, Lavender x 2, Off White x 12

▶ **Row 72:** Off White x 13, Lavender x 1, Off White x 18

◀ **Row 73:** Off White x 31

▶ **Row 74:** Off White x 30

◀ **Row 75:** Off White x 29

▶ **Row 76:** Off White x 28

◀ **Row 77:** Off White x 27

▶ **Row 78:** Off White x 26

◀ **Row 79:** Off White x 25

▶ **Row 80:** Off White x 24

◀ **Row 81:** Off White x 23

▶ **Row 82:** Off White x 22

◀ **Row 83:** Off White x 21

▶ **Row 84:** Off White x 20

◀ **Row 85:** Off White x 19

▶ **Row 86:** Off White x 18

◀ **Row 87:** Off White x 17

▶ **Row 88:** Off White x 16

◀ **Row 89:** Off White x 15

▶ **Row 90:** Off White x 14

◀ **Row 91:** Off White x 13

▶ **Row 92:** Off White x 12

◀ **Row 93:** Off White x 11

▶ **Row 94:** Off White x 10

◀ **Row 95:** Off White x 9

▶ **Row 96:** Off White x 8

◀ **Row 97:** Off White x 7

▶ **Row 98:** Off White x 6

◀ **Row 99:** Off White x 5

▶ **Row 100:** Off White x 4

◀ **Row 101:** Off White x 3

▶ **Row 102:** Off White x 2

◀ **Row 103:** Off White x 1

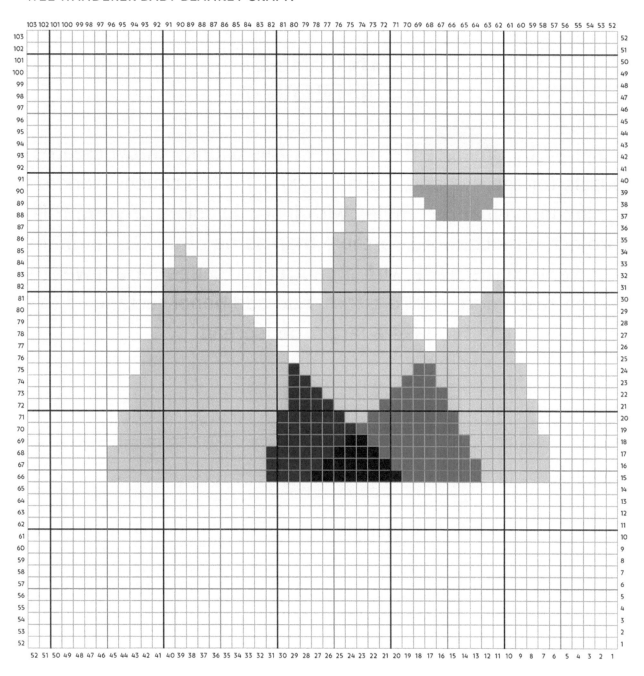

 Caron Simply Soft – Off White

Caron Simply Soft – Plum Perfect

Caron Simply Soft – Kelly Green

Caron Simply Soft – Persimmon

Caron Simply Soft – Chartreuse

Caron Simply Soft – Ocean

Caron Simply Soft – Robin's Egg Blue

Caron Simply Soft – Lavender Blue

Caron Simply Soft – Gold

Caron Simply Soft – Sunshine

INVERSE
THROW

Inspired by timeless tile patterns, this chunky throw creates a puzzle for the eye and a dose of cozy for the couch. Worked in nine individual rectangles with just two colors of yarn, this project is much more portable than some other C2C afghans. Replace the black with a neutral like taupe for a lower contrast, more subtle effect. Add additional rectangles to make a larger bedspread.

Difficulty Rating

Yarn

Lion Brand Wool-Ease Thick & Quick Bonus Bundle (80% acrylic, 20% wool), 6 super bulky (super chunky), 340g (212yd/193m), in the following shades:

› Black (153); 4 skeins

› Fisherman (098); 4 skeins

Supplies

Size P (11.5mm) hook

Finished Size

52 x 62in (132 x 157.5cm)

Gauge (Tension)

4 tiles measure $6^{1}/_{4}$in (16cm) using Size P (11.5mm) hook and Lion Brand Wool-Ease Thick & Quick Bonus Bundle

Stitch

Double crochet (UK treble crochet) C2C

Instructions

TO MAKE THE THROW

› Follow the written pattern and graph to make four #1 Rectangles and five #2 Rectangles. Leave a 25in (10cm) Black tail on each rectangle.

› Weave in all ends, except the 25in (10cm) tails.

› With a tapestry needle and leftover Black tails when possible, join rectangles using mattress stitch (see General Techniques: Mattress Stitch). Pull working yarn snug so as to best hide seam.

> Work with multiple balls of each color at the same time to avoid cutting yarn at each color change.

TIP

Join four rectangles to create a graphic, modern baby play mat.

RECTANGLE #1

Pattern

◀ **Row 1 [RS]:** White x 1

▶ **Row 2 [WS]:** White x 1, Black x 1

◀ **Row 3:** Black x 1, White x 2

▶ **Row 4:** Black x 1, White x 1, Black x 2

◀ **Row 5:** White x 1, Black x 1, White x 2, Black x 1

▶ **Row 6:** (Black x 2, White x 1) twice

◀ **Row 7:** White x 2, Black x 1, White x 2, Black x 2

▶ **Row 8:** Black x 3, White x 1, Black x 2, White x 2

◀ **Row 9:** White x 3, Black x 1, White x 5

▶ **Row 10:** White x 5, Black x 5

◀ **Row 11:** Black x 5, White x 6

CORNER *(decrease at beginning of WS row, increase at beginning of RS row)*

▶ **Row 12 [WS]:** Black x 11

◀ **Row 13 [RS]:** White x 6, Black x 5

CORNER *(decrease at beginning of each row)*

▶ **Row 14 [WS]:** Black x 5, White x 5

◀ **Row 15 [RS]:** White x 5, Black x 1, White x 3

▶ **Row 16:** White x 2, Black x 2, White x 1, Black x 3

◀ **Row 17:** Black x 2, White x 2, Black x 1, White x 2

▶ **Row 18:** (White x 1, Black x 2) twice

◀ **Row 19:** Black x 1, White x 2, Black x 1, White x 1

▶ **Row 20:** Black x 2, White x 1, Black x 1

◀ **Row 21:** White x 2, Black x 1

▶ **Row 22:** Black x 1, White x 1

◀ **Row 23:** White x 1

RECTANGLE #2

Pattern

◀ **Row 1 [RS]:** Black x 1

▶ **Row 2 [WS]:** Black x 1, White x 1

◀ **Row 3:** White x 1, Black x 2

▶ **Row 4:** White x 1, Black x 1, White x 2

◀ **Row 5:** Black x 1, White x 1, Black x 2, White x 1

▶ **Row 6:** (White x 2, Black x 1) twice

◀ **Row 7:** Black x 2, White x 1, Black x 2, White x 2

▶ **Row 8:** White x 3, Black x 1, White x 2, Black x 2

◀ **Row 9:** Black x 3, White x 1, Black x 5

▶ **Row 10:** Black x 5, White x 5

◀ **Row 11:** White x 5, Black x 6

CORNER *(decrease at beginning of WS row, increase at beginning of RS row)*

▶ **Row 12 [WS]:** White x 11

◀ **Row 13 [RS]:** Black x 6, White x 5

CORNER *(decrease at beginning of each row)*

▶ **Row 14 [WS]:** White x 5, Black x 5

◀ **Row 15 [RS]:** Black x 5, White x 1, Black x 3

▶ **Row 16:** Black x 2, White x 2, Black x 1, White x 3

◀ **Row 17:** White x 2, Black x 2, White x 1, Black x 2

▶ **Row 18:** (Black x 1, White x 2) twice

◀ **Row 19:** White x 1, Black x 2, White x 1, Black x 1

▶ **Row 20:** White x 2, Black x 1, White x 1

◀ **Row 21:** Black x 2, White x 1

▶ **Row 22:** White x 1, Black x 1

◀ **Row 23:** Black x 1

INVERSE THROW GRAPHS

Rectangle #1 Graph

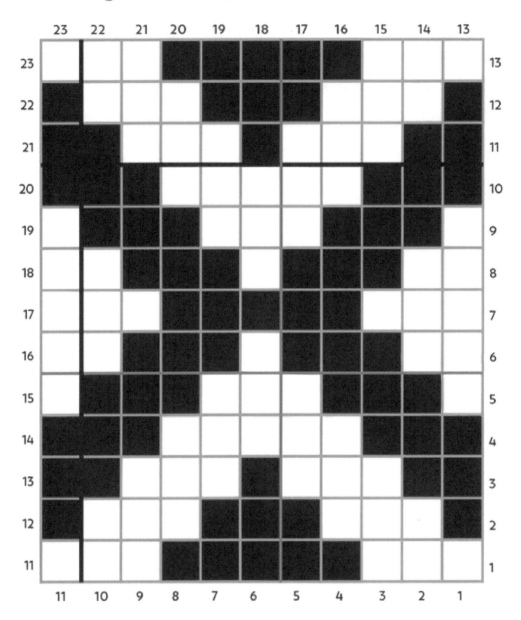

Rectangle #2 Graph

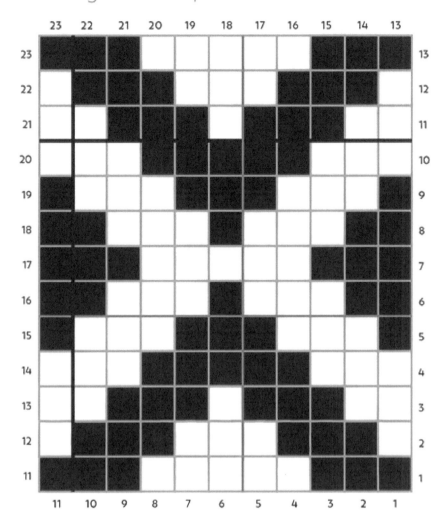

Lion Brand Wool-Ease Thick & Quick Bonus Bundle – Fisherman

Lion Brand Wool-Ease Thick & Quick Bonus Bundle – Black

Once all nine rectangles are complete, seam them as pictured into three vertical columns using mattress stitch (see General Techniques: Mattress Stitch). Then join the three columns using the same method.

FROSTED WINDOW
THROW

Let the yarn do the work in this beginner-friendly throw. By using a yarn with a variety of textures per skein, you'll be left with a substantial C2C blanket with very few ends to weave in. The pattern as written creates a large afghan, but you can crochet four rectangles in any size you wish to achieve the same visual effect at a different scale. Similarly, try a non-textured self-striping yarn to create a color-centric design.

Difficulty Rating

Yarn

Bernat Mix Home (60% acrylic, 18% cotton, 13% nylon, 7% wool, 2% polyester), 6 super bulky (16-ply, super chunky), 225g (183yd/167m), in the following shade:

> In the Clouds; 10 skeins

Supplies

Size N (10mm) hook

Finished Size

47 x 56in (119.5 x 142cm)

Gauge (Tension)

4 tiles measure $4^1/_4$in (11cm) using size N (10mm) hook and Bernat Mix Home

Stitch

Double crochet (UK treble crochet) C2C

NOTES

◢ If you desire a different size blanket than listed, use the gauge listed to determine how many tiles to work for the width and height of each rectangle in order to achieve the size you'd like.

Instructions

TO MAKE THE THROW

> Follow the written pattern and graph to crochet four identical rectangles.

> For joining, sew rectangles in orientation pictured (see General Techniques: Joining C2C Pieces).

> For the border, work as described below. You may find that the transitions between yarn textures make the border look uneven. In this case, simply cut yarn so that only one texture is used per border side.

Border Round 1: Work one round of single crochet border (see General Techniques: Single Crochet Border).

Border Round 2: Ch 1, sc in first sc, *2 dc in next ch2sp, sc in next sc; repeat from * to beginning of round, working 2 sc in both sc sts at each corner, slst to first sc of round to join. Fasten off.

Weave in ends.

TIP

Try joining the rectangles in other orientations too–it'll really change the look of your project!

Pattern

◀ **Row 1 [RS]:** Clouds x 1

▶ **Row 2 [WS]:** Clouds x 2

◀ **Row 3:** Clouds x 3

▶ **Row 4:** Clouds x 4

◀ **Row 5:** Clouds x 5

▶ **Row 6:** Clouds x 6

◀ **Row 7:** Clouds x 7

▶ **Row 8:** Clouds x 8

◀ **Row 9:** Clouds x 9

▶ **Row 10:** Clouds x 10

◀ **Row 11:** Clouds x 11

▶ **Row 12:** Clouds x 12

◀ **Row 13:** Clouds x 13

▶ **Row 14:** Clouds x 14

◀ **Row 15:** Clouds x 15

▶ **Row 16:** Clouds x 16

◀ **Row 17:** Clouds x 17

▶ **Row 18:** Clouds x 18

◀ **Row 19:** Clouds x 19

▶ **Row 20:** Clouds x 20

CORNER *(increase at beginning of RS row, decrease at beginning of WS row)*

◀ **Row 21 [RS]:** Clouds x 20

▶ **Row 22 [WS]:** Clouds x 20

◀ **Row 23:** Clouds x 20

▶ **Row 24:** Clouds x 20

CORNER *(decrease at beginning of each row)*

◀ **Row 25 [RS]:** Clouds x 19

▶ **Row 26 [WS]:** Clouds x 18

◀ **Row 27:** Clouds x 17

▶ **Row 28:** Clouds x 16

◀ **Row 29:** Clouds x 15

▶ **Row 30:** Clouds x 14

◀ **Row 31:** Clouds x 13

▶ **Row 32:** Clouds x 12

◀ **Row 33:** Clouds x 11

▶ **Row 34:** Clouds x 10

◀ **Row 35:** Clouds x 9

▶ **Row 36:** Clouds x 8

◀ **Row 37:** Clouds x 7

▶ **Row 38:** Clouds x 6

◀ **Row 39:** Clouds x 5

▶ **Row 40:** Clouds x 4

◀ **Row 41:** Clouds x 3

▶ **Row 42:** Clouds x 2

◀ **Row 43:** Clouds x 1

FROSTED WINDOW THROW GRAPH

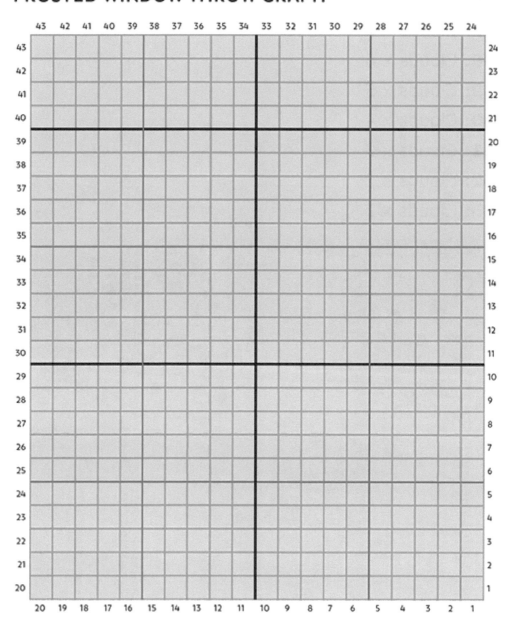

Bernat Mix Home – In the Clouds

SKI LODGE
PILLOW

Even if you spend winters far from the Swiss Alps, this Nordic-inspired snowflake pillow will add a good splash of hygge to your couch, chair or bed. Make it in colors to accent your Christmas décor or a neutral palette that you can enjoy all winter long. Because the yarn carries can be hidden inside the pillow, there are deceptively few tails to weave in at the end.

Difficulty Rating

Yarn

Lion Brand Vanna's Choice (100% acrylic), 4 worsted (10-ply/aran), 100g (170yd/156m), in the following shades:

> Graphite (407); 4 skeins

> Pearl Mist (305); 3 skeins

> Cranberry (180); 1 skein

Supplies

Size G (4mm) hook

22 x 22in (56 x 56cm) pillow insert

Finished Size

$21^1/_2$x $21^1/_2$in (54.5 x 54.5cm) before stuffing

Gauge (Tension)

4 tiles measure $2^3/_4$in (7cm) using size G (4mm) hook and Lion Brand Vanna's Choice

Stitch

Double crochet (UK treble crochet) C2C

NOTES

◢ *This pattern is a great opportunity to practice using small clip bobbins, like the ones pictured in Tools and Materials. This way, you can work with several balls of Graphite and Pearl Mist at the same time, keeping them clipped to your project until it's their turn to be used. If this feels too cumbersome, clip them all to a clothes hanger and hang it near your work area.*

◢ When switching colors, feel free to take liberties when picking up a strand of yarn that was used elsewhere in the design. Once the pillow is seamed, any picked up strands will be hidden inside! Just be certain to only carry yarn across on the WS of the piece.

◢ Similarly, unless it'll drive you crazy to know they're there, just tuck the yarn ends inside the pillow and seam it closed. Less weaving in = more crochet time!

Instructions

TO MAKE THE PILLOW

› Follow the written pattern and graphs to crochet a pillow front and a pillow back.

› For joining, with RS facing out, pin pillow front and back together.

› Using Pearl Mist, sc around three sides of pillow working through both the front and back of the pillow and working an extra sc in each corner.

› Insert pillow form.

› Sc along final side to join front and back. Slst to first sc to join.

› Weave in any remaining ends.

› For the border, using Cranberry (or Graphite for a more neutral look), work one round of crab stitch border (see General Techniques: Crab Stitch Border) around pillow.

› Fasten off and weave in any remaining ends.

TIP

For a larger pillow or floor cushion, work the graphs using a heavier yarn and larger hook. To make a smaller pillow, use the recommended yarn and hook with a half double crochet stitch.

Pattern

FRONT OF PILLOW

◀ **Row 1 [RS]:** Pearl x 1

▶ **Row 2 [WS]:** Pearl x 2

◀ **Row 3:** Pearl x 3

▶ **Row 4:** Pearl x 4

◀ **Row 5:** Pearl x 5

▶ **Row 6:** Pearl x 6

◀ **Row 7:** Pearl x 3, Graphite x 1, Pearl x 3

▶ **Row 8:** Pearl x 8

◀ **Row 9:** Pearl x 4, Graphite x 1, Pearl x 4

▶ **Row 10:** Pearl x 10

◀ **Row 11:** Pearl x 3, Graphite x 5, Pearl x 3

▶ **Row 12:** Pearl x 12

◀ **Row 13:** Pearl x 4, Graphite x 5, Pearl x 4

▶ **Row 14:** Pearl x 3, Graphite x 1, Pearl x 6, Graphite x 1, Pearl x 3

◀ **Row 15:** Pearl x 4, Graphite x 1, Pearl x 2, Graphite x 1, Pearl x 2, Graphite x 1, Pearl x 4

▶ **Row 16:** Pearl x 4, Graphite x 2, Pearl x 4, Graphite x 2, Pearl x 4

◀ **Row 17:** Pearl x 6, Graphite x 1, Pearl x 1, Graphite x 1, Pearl x 1, Graphite x 1, Pearl x 6

▶ **Row 18:** Pearl x 5, Graphite x 3, Pearl x 2, Graphite x 3, Pearl x 5

◀ **Row 19:** Pearl x 7, Graphite x 5, Pearl x 7

▶ **Row 20:** Pearl x 6, Graphite x 3, Pearl x 2, Graphite x 3, Pearl x 6

◀ **Row 21:** Pearl x 8, Graphite x 5, Pearl x 8

▶ **Row 22:** Pearl x 7, Graphite x 3, Pearl x 2, Graphite x 3, Pearl x 7

◀ **Row 23:** Pearl x 9, Graphite x 5, Pearl x 9

▶ **Row 24:** Pearl x 3, Graphite x 8, Pearl x 2, Graphite x 8, Pearl x 3

◀ **Row 25:** Pearl x 4, Graphite x 1, Pearl x 5, Graphite x 5, Pearl x 5, Graphite x 1, Pearl x 4

▶ **Row 26:** Pearl x 5, Graphite x 5, Pearl x 1, Graphite x 1, Pearl x 2, Graphite x 1, Pearl x 1, Graphite x 5, Pearl x 5

◀ **Row 27:** Pearl x 3, Graphite x 2, Pearl x 1, Graphite x 5, Pearl x 1, Graphite x 3, Pearl x 1, Graphite x 5, Pearl x 1, Graphite x 2, Pearl x 3

▶ **Row 28:** Pearl x 7, Graphite x 5, Pearl x 4, Graphite x 5, Pearl x 7

◀ **Row 29:** Pearl x 4, Graphite x 2, Pearl x 2, Graphite x 5, Pearl x 1, Graphite x 1, Pearl x 1, Graphite x 5, Pearl x 2, Graphite x 2, Pearl x 4

▶ **Row 30:** Pearl x 30

◀ **Row 31:** Pearl x 3, Graphite x 25, Pearl x 3

CORNER *(decrease at beginning of each row)*

▶ **Row 32 [WS]:** Pearl x 30

◀ **Row 33 [RS]:** Pearl x 4, Graphite x 2, Pearl x 2, Graphite x 5, Pearl x 1, Graphite x 1, Pearl x 1, Graphite x 5, Pearl x 2, Graphite x 2, Pearl x 4

▶ **Row 34:** Pearl x 7, Graphite x 5, Pearl x 4, Graphite x 5, Pearl x 7

◀ **Row 35:** Pearl x 3, Graphite x 2, Pearl x 1, Graphite x 5, Pearl x 1, Graphite x 3, Pearl x 1, Graphite x 5, Pearl x 1, Graphite x 2, Pearl x 3

▶ **Row 36:** Pearl x 5, Graphite x 5, Pearl x 1, Graphite x 1, Pearl x 2, Graphite x 1, Pearl x 1, Graphite x 5, Pearl x 5

◀ **Row 37:** Pearl x 4, Graphite x 1, Pearl x 5, Graphite x 5, Pearl x 5, Graphite x 1, Pearl x 4

▶ **Row 38:** Pearl x 3, Graphite x 8, Pearl x 2, Graphite x 8, Pearl x 3

◀ **Row 39:** Pearl x 9, Graphite x 5, Pearl x 9

▶ **Row 40:** Pearl x 7, Graphite x 3, Pearl x 2, Graphite x 3, Pearl x 7

◀ **Row 41:** Pearl x 8, Graphite x 5, Pearl x 8

▶ **Row 42:** Pearl x 6, Graphite x 3, Pearl x 2, Graphite x 3, Pearl x 6

◀ **Row 43:** Pearl x 7, Graphite x 5, Pearl x 7

▶ **Row 44:** Pearl x 5, Graphite x 3, Pearl x 2, Graphite x 3, Pearl x 5

◀ **Row 45:** Pearl x 6, Graphite x 1, Pearl x 1, Graphite x 1, Pearl x 1, Graphite x 1, Pearl x 6

▶ **Row 46:** Pearl x 4, Graphite x 2, Pearl x 4, Graphite x 2, Pearl x 4

◀ **Row 47:** Pearl x 4, Graphite x 1, Pearl x 2, Graphite x 1, Pearl x 2, Graphite x 1, Pearl x 4

▶ **Row 48:** Pearl x 3, Graphite x 1, Pearl x 6, Graphite x 1, Pearl x 3

◀ **Row 49:** Pearl x 4, Graphite x 5, Pearl x 4

▶ **Row 50:** Pearl x 12

◀ **Row 51:** Pearl x 3, Graphite x 5, Pearl x 3

▶ **Row 52:** Pearl x 10

◀ **Row 53:** Pearl x 4, Graphite x 1, Pearl x 4

▶ **Row 54:** Pearl x 8

◀ **Row 55:** Pearl x 3, Graphite x 1, Pearl x 3

▶ **Row 56:** Pearl x 6

◀ **Row 57:** Pearl x 5

▶ **Row 58:** Pearl x 4

◀ **Row 59:** Pearl x 3

▶ **Row 60:** Pearl x 2

◀ **Row 61:** Pearl x 1

BACK OF PILLOW

◀ **Row 1 [RS]:** Graphite x 1

▶ **Row 2 [WS]:** Graphite x 2

◀ **Row 3:** Graphite x 3

▶ **Row 4:** Graphite x 4

◀ **Row 5:** Graphite x 5

▶ **Row 6:** Graphite x 6

◀ **Row 7:** Graphite x 7

▶ **Row 8:** Graphite x 8

◀ **Row 9:** Graphite x 9

▶ **Row 10:** Graphite x 10

◀ **Row 11:** Graphite x 11

▶ **Row 12:** Graphite x 12

◀ **Row 13:** Graphite x 13

▶ **Row 14:** Graphite x 14

◀ **Row 15:** Graphite x 15

▶ **Row 16:** Graphite x 16

◀ **Row 17:** Graphite x 17

▶ **Row 18:** Graphite x 18

◀ **Row 19:** Graphite x 19

▶ **Row 20:** Graphite x 20

◀ **Row 21:** Graphite x 21

▶ **Row 22:** Graphite x 22

◀ **Row 23:** Graphite x 23

▶ **Row 24:** Graphite x 24

◀ **Row 25:** Graphite x 25

▶ **Row 26:** Graphite x 26

◀ **Row 27:** Graphite x 27

▶ **Row 28:** Graphite x 28

◀ **Row 29:** Graphite x 29

▶ **Row 30:** Graphite x 30

◀ **Row 31:** Graphite x 31

CORNER *(decrease at beginning of each row)*

▶ **Row 32 [WS]:** Graphite x 30

◀ **Row 33 [RS]:** Graphite x 29

▶ **Row 34:** Graphite x 28

◀ **Row 35:** Graphite x 27

▶ **Row 36:** Graphite x 26

◀ **Row 37:** Graphite x 25

▶ **Row 38:** Graphite x 24

◀ **Row 39:** Graphite x 23

▶ **Row 40:** Graphite x 22

◀ **Row 41:** Graphite x 21

▶ **Row 42:** Graphite x 20

◀ **Row 43:** Graphite x 19

▶ **Row 44:** Graphite x 18

◀ **Row 45:** Graphite x 17

▶ **Row 46:** Graphite x 16

◀ **Row 47:** Graphite x 15

▶ **Row 48:** Graphite x 14

◀ **Row 49:** Graphite x 13

▶ **Row 50:** Graphite x 12

◀ **Row 51:** Graphite x 11

▶ **Row 52:** Graphite x 10

◀ **Row 53:** Graphite x 9

▶ **Row 54:** Graphite x 8

◀ **Row 55:** Graphite x 7

▶ **Row 56:** Graphite x 6

◀ **Row 57:** Graphite x 5

▶ **Row 58:** Graphite x 4

◀ **Row 59:** Graphite x 3

▶ **Row 60:** Graphite x 2

◀ **Row 61:** Graphite x 1

SKI LODGE PILLOW GRAPH – FRONT

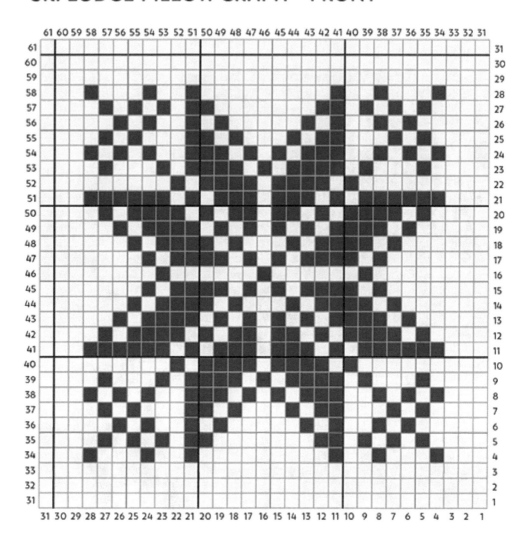

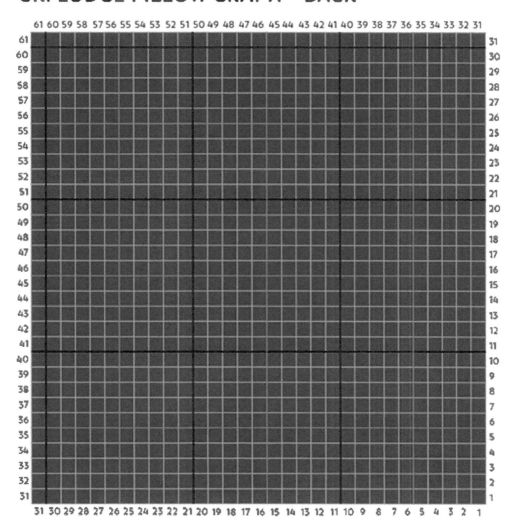

 Lion Brand Vanna's Choice – Graphite

Lion Brand Vanna's Choice – Pearl Mist

DOWN SHIFT
BICYCLE PILLOW

Perfect for an office, nursery or living room, you'll cruise through this manageably-sized pillow pattern faster than you can say "kick stand". Half double crochet stitches are used to create more detail in the pillow, but if you'd prefer a larger cushion, double crochet stitches can be easily substituted.

Difficulty Rating

Yarn

Lion Brand Heartland Solids (100% acrylic), 4 worsted (10-ply/aran), 142g (251yd/230m), in the following shade:

> Cuyahoga Valley (171); 2 skeins

Lion Brand Heartland Prints (100% acrylic), 4 worsted (10-ply/aran), 113g (200yd/183m), in the following shade:

> Mount Rainier Tweed (350); 2 skeins

Supplies

Size G (4mm) hook

12 x 20in (30 x 51cm) pillow insert

Finished Size

12 x 19$\frac{1}{2}$in (30 x 49.5cm) before stuffing

Gauge (Tension)

4 tiles measure 2$\frac{3}{4}$in (7cm) using size G (4mm) hook and Lion Brand Heartland

Stitch

Half double crochet (UK half treble crochet) C2C

NOTES

◢ When switching colors, feel free to take liberties when picking up a strand of yarn that was used elsewhere in the design. Once the pillow is seamed, any picked up strands will be hidden inside! Just be certain to only carry yarn across on the WS of the piece.

◢ Similarly, unless it'll drive you crazy to know they're there, just tuck the yarn ends inside the pillow and seam it closed. Less weaving in =

Instructions

TO MAKE THE PILLOW

› Follow the written pattern and graphs to crochet a pillow front and back.

› For joining, with RS facing out, pin pillow front and back together. Using one strand of Valley colored yarn, sc around three sides of pillow working through both the front and back of the pillow. Work an extra sc in each corner.

› Insert pillow form.

› Sc along final side to join front and back. Slst to first sc to join.

› Weave in any remaining ends.

Pattern

FRONT OF PILLOW

◀ **Row 1 [RS]:** Tweed x 1

▶ **Row 2 [WS]:** Tweed x 2

◀ **Row 3:** Tweed x 3

▶ **Row 4:** Tweed x 4

◀ **Row 5:** Tweed x 5

▶ **Row 6:** Tweed x 6

◀ **Row 7:** Tweed x 2, Valley x 3, Tweed x 2

▶ **Row 8:** Tweed x 2, Valley x 4, Tweed x 2

◀ **Row 9:** Tweed x 2, Valley x 1, Tweed x 3, Valley x 1, Tweed x 2

▶ **Row 10:** Tweed x 2, Valley x 1, Tweed x 4, Valley x 1, Tweed x 2

◀ **Row 11:** Tweed x 2, Valley x 1, Tweed x 5, Valley x 1, Tweed x 2

▶ **Row 12:** Tweed x 3, Valley x 1, Tweed x 4, Valley x 1, Tweed x 3

◀ **Row 13:** Tweed x 3, Valley x 1, (Tweed x 2, Valley x 1) twice, Tweed x 3

▶ **Row 14:** (Tweed x 4, Valley x 1) twice, Tweed x 4

◀ **Row 15:** Tweed x 4, Valley x 1, (Tweed x 2, Valley x 1) twice, Tweed x 4

▶ **Row 16:** Tweed x 5, Valley x 1, Tweed x 4, Valley x 1, Tweed x 5

◀ **Row 17:** Tweed x 6, (Valley x 1, Tweed x 1) twice, Valley x 1, Tweed x 6

▶ **Row 18:** Tweed x 7, Valley x 4, Tweed x 7

◀ **Row 19:** Tweed x 8, Valley x 3, Tweed x 2, Valley x 1, Tweed x 5

CORNER *(increase at beginning of WS rows, decrease at beginning of RS rows)*

▶ **Row 20 [WS]:** Tweed x 5, Valley x 1, Tweed x 13

134

◀ **Row 21 [RS]:** Tweed x 8, Valley x 1, Tweed x 2, Valley x 3, Tweed x 5

▶ **Row 22:** Tweed x 8, Valley x 2, Tweed x 9

◀ **Row 23:** Tweed x 4, Valley x 1, Tweed x 2, Valley x 2, Tweed x 2, Valley x 1, Tweed x 7

▶ **Row 24:** Tweed x 2, Valley x 3, Tweed x 7, Valley x 4, Tweed x 3

◀ **Row 25:** Tweed x 3, Valley x 2, Tweed x 1, Valley x 1, Tweed x 3, Valley x 1, Tweed x 2, Valley x 4, Tweed x 2

▶ **Row 26:** Tweed x 2, Valley x 1, Tweed x 3, Valley x 1, Tweed x 5, Valley x 1, Tweed x 1, Valley x 2, Tweed x 3

◀ **Row 27:** Tweed x 6, Valley x 1, Tweed x 2, Valley x 1, Tweed x 1, Valley x 1, Tweed x 4, Valley x 1, Tweed x 2

▶ **Row 28:** Tweed x 2, Valley x 1, Tweed x 5, Valley x 1, Tweed x 3, Valley x 1, Tweed x 6

◀ **Row 29:** Tweed x 6, (Valley x 1, Tweed x 1) twice, Valley x 1, Tweed x 4, Valley x 1, Tweed x 3

▶ **Row 30:** Tweed x 3, (Valley x 1, Tweed x 2) 3 times, Valley x 1, Tweed x 6

CORNER *(decrease at beginning of each row)*

◀ **Row 31 [RS]:** Tweed x 4, Valley x 1, Tweed x 1, Valley x 2, Tweed x 1, Valley x 3, Tweed x 2, Valley x 1, Tweed x 3

▶ **Row 32 [WS]:** Tweed x 2, Valley x 1, Tweed x 4, Valley x 2, (Tweed x 1, Valley x 1) twice, Tweed x 4

◀ **Row 33:** Tweed x 2, (Valley x 1, Tweed x 1) twice, Valley x 3, Tweed x 4, Valley x 1, Tweed x 2

▶ **Row 34:** Tweed x 2, Valley x 1, Tweed x 3, Valley x 1, Tweed x 1, Valley x 3, Tweed x 1, Valley x 1, Tweed x 2

◀ **Row 35:** Tweed x 2, Valley x 1, Tweed x 1, Valley x 2, Tweed x 2, Valley x 4, Tweed x 2

▶ **Row 36:** Tweed x 2, Valley x 3, Tweed x 3, Valley x 3, Tweed x 2

◀ **Row 37:** Tweed x 12

▶ **Row 38:** Tweed x 11

◀ **Row 39:** Tweed x 10

▶ **Row 40:** Tweed x 9

◀ **Row 41:** Tweed x 8

▶ **Row 42:** Tweed x 7

◀ **Row 43:** Tweed x 6

▶ **Row 44:** Tweed x 5

◀ **Row 45:** Tweed x 4

▶ **Row 46:** Tweed x 3

◀ **Row 47:** Tweed x 2

▶ **Row 48:** Tweed x 1

BACK OF PILLOW

◀ **Row 1 [RS]:** Valley x 1

▶ **Row 2 [WS]:** Valley x 2

◀ **Row 3:** Valley x 3

▶ **Row 4:** Valley x 4

◀ **Row 5:** Valley x 5

▶ **Row 6:** Valley x 6

◀ **Row 7:** Valley x 7

▶ **Row 8:** Valley x 8

◀ **Row 9:** Valley x 9

▶ **Row 10:** Valley x 10

◀ **Row 11:** Valley x 11

▶ **Row 12:** Valley x 12

◀ **Row 13:** Valley x 13

▶ **Row 14:** Valley x 14

◀ **Row 15:** Valley x 15

▶ **Row 16:** Valley x 16

◀ **Row 17:** Valley x 17

▶ **Row 18:** Valley x 18

◀ **Row 19:** Valley x 19

CORNER *(increase at beginning of ws rows, decrease at beginning of rs rows)*

▶ **Row 20 [WS]:** Valley x 19

◀ **Row 21 [RS]:** Valley x 19

▶ **Row 22:** Valley x 19

◀ **Row 23:** Valley x 19

▶ **Row 24:** Valley x 19

◀ **Row 25:** Valley x 19

▶ **Row 26:** Valley x 19

◀ **Row 27:** Valley x 19

▶ **Row 28:** Valley x 19

◀ **Row 29:** Valley x 19

▶ **Row 30:** Valley x 19

CORNER *(decrease at beginning of each row)*

◀ **Row 31 [RS]:** Valley x 18

▶ **Row 32 [WS]:** Valley x 17

◀ **Row 33:** Valley x 16

▶ **Row 34:** Valley x 15

◀ **Row 35:** Valley x 14

▶ **Row 36:** Valley x 13

◀ **Row 37:** Valley x 12

▶ **Row 38:** Valley x 11

◀ **Row 39:** Valley x 10

▶ **Row 40:** Valley x 9

◀ **Row 41:** Valley x 8

▶ **Row 42:** Valley x 7

◀ **Row 43:** Valley x 6

▶ **Row 44:** Valley x 5

◀ **Row 45:** Valley x 4

▶ **Row 46:** Valley x 3

◀ **Row 47:** Valley x 2

▶ **Row 48:** Valley x 1

TIP

Wind off multiple balls of each color before starting to avoid cutting yarn at each color change. Try using clip bobbins as described in Tips for Wrangling Your Yarns (see Managing Yarns), to keep the small balls organized while you work.

DOWN SHIFT BICYCLE PILLOW GRAPH – FRONT

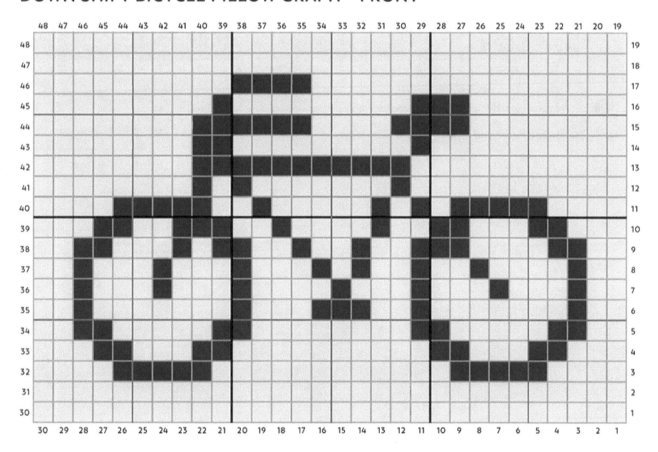

DOWN SHIFT BICYCLE PILLOW GRAPH – BACK

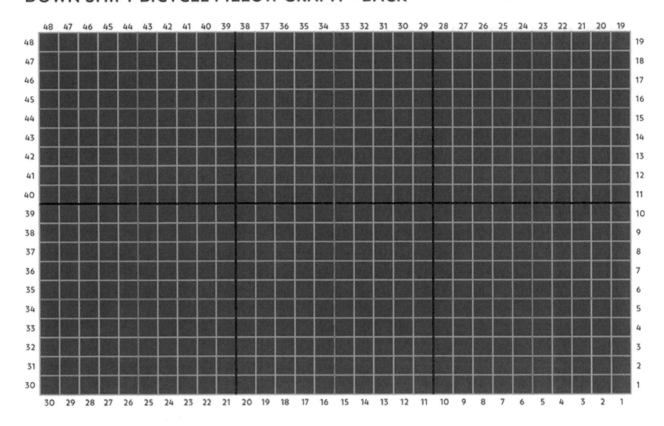

⬤ *Lion Brand Heartland Solids – Cuyahoga Valley*

◯ *Lion Brand Heartland Prints – Mount Rainier Tweed*

TAPESTRY PILLOW

C2C is a great way to replicate the look of graphic woven textiles with crochet. This Tapestry Pillow pays homage to traditional geometric kilim rugs and with its simplified color palette it will look at home in any room. Use a bulkier yarn and larger hook to create an even bigger floor cushion. For a simple beginner project with beautiful texture, make two solid-colored squares by following the instructions for the back.

Difficulty Rating

Yarn

Lion Brand Vanna's Choice (100% acrylic), 4 worsted (10-ply/aran), 100g (170yd/156m), in the following shades:

› Toffee (124); 3 skeins

› Linen (099); 6 skeins

Supplies

Size H (5mm) hook

20in (51cm) pillow insert

Finished Size

20 x 20in (51 x 51cm)

Gauge (Tension)

4 tiles measure $3^1/_2$in (9cm), using size H (5mm) hook and Lion Brand Vanna's Choice

Stitch

Double crochet (UK treble crochet) C2C

NOTES

◢ *Pillow front and back are worked with two strands of yarn held together throughout.*

◢ *Divide the third skein of Toffee into two balls to work the final section of the graph.*

◢ *Unless it'll drive you crazy to know they're there, just tuck the yarn ends inside the pillow and seam it closed. Less weaving in = more crochet time!*

Instructions

TO MAKE THE PILLOW

❯ Follow the written pattern and graphs to crochet a pillow front and a pillow back.

❯ Block pillow front and back to ensure they're the same size.

❯ If desired, use a tapestry needle and Linen yarn to visually "connect" any of the Linen tiles whose corners are separated by a strand of Toffee yarn.

❯ With RS facing out, pin pillow front and back together. Using two strands of Toffee yarn held together, sc around three sides of pillow working through both the front and back of the pillow. Work an extra sc in each corner.

❯ Insert pillow form. Sc along final side to join front and back, slst to first sc to join. Weave in any remaining ends.

TIP

You may choose to tidy up the look of your pillow front by using small stitches of Linen colored yarn to connect some of the Linen tiles. Either use yarn ends that are there already or a fresh strand of Linen yarn (see Managing Yarns: How to Weave in Ends). on how to do this).

Pattern

FRONT OF PILLOW

◀ **Row 1 [RS]:** Toffee x 1

▶ **Row 2 [WS]:** Toffee x 2

◀ **Row 3:** Linen x 2, Toffee x 1

▶ **Row 4:** (Toffee x 1, Linen x 1) twice

◀ **Row 5:** Toffee x 1, Linen x 3, Toffee x 1

▶ **Row 6:** Toffee x 4, Linen x 1, Toffee x 1

◀ **Row 7:** Linen x 1, Toffee x 1, Linen x 4, Toffee x 1

► **Row 8:** Toffee x 2, Linen x 5, Toffee x 1

◄ **Row 9:** Toffee x 2, Linen x 1, Toffee x 3, Linen x 2, Toffee x 1

► **Row 10:** (Toffee x 1, Linen x 1) twice, Toffee x 2, Linen x 1, Toffee x 3

◄ **Row 11:** Linen x 3, Toffee x 1, Linen x 1, Toffee x 2, Linen x 3, Toffee x 1

► **Row 12:** Toffee x 4, Linen x 1, Toffee x 1, Linen x 1, Toffee x 2, Linen x 2, Toffee x 1

◄ **Row 13:** (Linen x 1, Toffee x 2) twice, Linen x 1, Toffee x 1, Linen x 4, Toffee x 1

► **Row 14:** Toffee x 2, Linen x 5, (Toffee x 1, Linen x 1) 3 times, Toffee x 1

◄ **Row 15:** Toffee x 1, Linen x 1, Toffee x 2, Linen x 1, Toffee x 3, Linen x 1, Toffee x 3, Linen x 2, Toffee x 1

► **Row 16:** (Toffee x 1, Linen x 1) twice, Toffee x 2, Linen x 1, Toffee x 5, Linen x 2, Toffee x 2

◄ **Row 17:** Linen x 1, Toffee x 1, Linen x 3, Toffee x 1, Linen x 3, Toffee x 1, Linen x 1, Toffee x 2, Linen x 3, Toffee x 1

► **Row 18:** Toffee x 4, Linen x 1, Toffee x 1, Linen x 1, Toffee x 2, Linen x 2, Toffee x 5, Linen x 1, Toffee x 1

◄ **Row 19:** Toffee x 2, Linen x 1, Toffee x 3, Linen x 1, (Toffee x 2, Linen x 1) twice, Toffee x 1, Linen x 4, Toffee x 1

► **Row 20:** Toffee x 2, Linen x 5, (Toffee x 1, Linen x 1) 4 times, Toffee x 1, Linen x 4

◄ **Row 21:** Linen x 3, Toffee x 1, Linen x 1, (Toffee x 2, Linen x 1) twice, Toffee x 3, Linen x 1, Toffee x 3, Linen x 2, Toffee x 1

► **Row 22:** (Toffee x 1, Linen x 1) twice, Toffee x 2, Linen x 1, Toffee x 5, Linen x 2, Toffee x 2, Linen x 1, Toffee x 1, Linen x 1, Toffee x 3

◄ **Row 23:** Toffee x 1, Linen x 3, Toffee x 2, Linen x 1, (Toffee x 1, Linen x 3) twice, Toffee x 1, Linen x 1, Toffee x 2, Linen x 3, Toffee x 1

CORNER *(decrease at beginning of each row)*

▶ **Row 24 [WS]:** Toffee x 3, Linen x 1, Toffee x 1, Linen x 1, Toffee x 2, Linen x 2, Toffee x 5, Linen x 1, Toffee x 2, (Linen x 1, Toffee x 1) twice

◀ **Row 25 [RS]:** Toffee x 1, Linen x 2, Toffee x 3, Linen x 1, Toffee x 3, Linen x 1, (Toffee x 2, Linen x 1) twice, Toffee x 1, Linen x 3

▶ **Row 26:** Linen x 4, (Toffee x 1, Linen x 1) 4 times, Toffee x 1, Linen x 5, Toffee x 2

◀ **Row 27:** Toffee x 1, Linen x 4, Toffee x 1, Linen x 1, (Toffee x 2, Linen x 1) twice, Toffee x 3, Linen x 1, Toffee x 2

▶ **Row 28:** Toffee x 1, Linen x 1, Toffee x 5, Linen x 2, Toffee x 2, Linen x 1, Toffee x 1, Linen x 1, Toffee x 4

◀ **Row 29:** Toffee x 1, Linen x 3, Toffee x 2, Linen x 1, (Toffee x 1, Linen x 3) twice, Toffee x 1, Linen x 1

▶ **Row 30:** Toffee x 2, Linen x 2, Toffee x 5, Linen x 1, Toffee x 2, (Linen x 1, Toffee x 1) twice

◀ **Row 31:** Toffee x 1, Linen x 2, (Toffee x 3, Linen x 1) twice, Toffee x 2, Linen x 1, Toffee x 1

▶ **Row 32:** (Toffee x 1, Linen x 1) 3 times, Toffee x 1, Linen x 5, Toffee x 2

◀ **Row 33:** Toffee x 1, Linen x 4, Toffee x 1, Linen x 1, (Toffee x 2, Linen x 1) twice

▶ **Row 34:** Toffee x 1, Linen x 2, Toffee x 2, Linen x 1, Toffee x 1, Linen x 1, Toffee x 4

◀ **Row 35:** Toffee x 1, Linen x 3, Toffee x 2, Linen x 1, Toffee x 1, Linen x 3

▶ **Row 36:** Toffee x 3, Linen x 1, Toffee x 2, (Linen x 1, Toffee x 1) twice

◀ **Row 37:** Toffee x 1, Linen x 2, Toffee x 3, Linen x 1, Toffee x 2

▶ **Row 38:** Toffee x 1, Linen x 5, Toffee x 2

◀ **Row 39:** Toffee x 1, Linen x 4, Toffee x 1, Linen x 1

▶ **Row 40:** Toffee x 1, Linen x 1, Toffee x 4

◀ **Row 41:** Toffee x 1, Linen x 3, Toffee x 1

▶ **Row 42:** (Linen x 1, Toffee x 1) twice

◀ **Row 43:** Toffee x 1, Linen x 2

▶ **Row 44:** Toffee x 2

◀ **Row 45:** Toffee x 1

BACK OF PILLOW

◀ **Row 1 [RS]:** Linen x 1

▶ **Row 2 [WS]:** Linen x 2

◀ **Row 3:** Linen x 3

▶ **Row 4:** Linen x 4

◀ **Row 5:** Linen x 5

▶ **Row 6:** Linen x 6

◀ **Row 7:** Linen x 7

▶ **Row 8:** Linen x 8

◀ **Row 9:** Linen x 9

▶ **Row 10:** Linen x 10

◀ **Row 11:** Linen x 11

▶ **Row 12:** Linen x 12

◀ **Row 13:** Linen x 13

▶ **Row 14:** Linen x 14

◀ **Row 15:** Linen x 15

▶ **Row 16:** Linen x 16

◀ **Row 17:** Linen x 17

▶ **Row 18:** Linen x 18

◀ **Row 19:** Linen x 19

▶ **Row 20:** Linen x 20

◀ **Row 21:** Linen x 21

▶ **Row 22:** Linen x 22

◀ **Row 23:** Linen x 23

CORNER *(decrease at beginning of each row)*

▶ **Row 24 [WS]:** Linen x 22

◀ **Row 25 [RS]:** Linen x 21

▶ **Row 26:** Linen x 20

◀ **Row 27:** Linen x 19

▶ **Row 28:** Linen x 18

◀ **Row 29:** Linen x 17

▶ **Row 30:** Linen x 16

◀ **Row 31:** Linen x 15

▶ **Row 32:** Linen x 14

◀ **Row 33:** Linen x 13

▶ **Row 34:** Linen x 12

◀ **Row 35:** Linen x 11

▶ **Row 36:** Linen x 10

◀ **Row 37:** Linen x 9

▶ **Row 38:** Linen x 8

◀ **Row 39:** Linen x 7

▶ **Row 40:** Linen x 6

◀ **Row 41:** Linen x 5

▶ **Row 42:** Linen x 4

◀ **Row 43:** Linen x 3

▶ **Row 44:** Linen x 2

◀ **Row 45:** Linen x 1

TAPESTRY PILLOW GRAPH – BACK

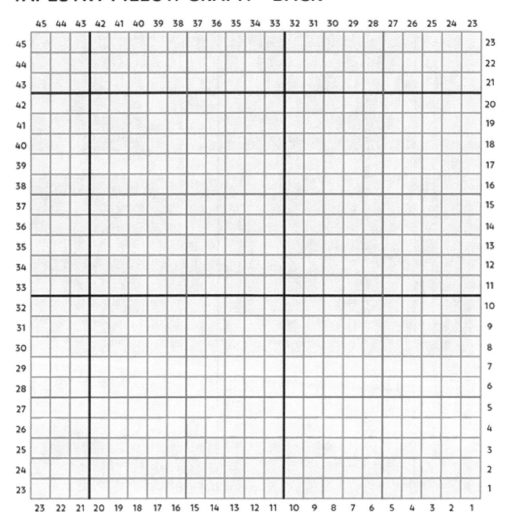

Lion Brand Vanna's Choice - Toffee

Lion Brand Vanna's Choice - Linen

LOVE SQUARED
WASHCLOTH

When you need a hostess gift or a stocking stuffer in a jiffy, this charming washcloth can be crocheted in a little over an hour. Make it in taupe and ecru for a farmhouse style washcloth or brighter colors for a more playful look. If you favor decorative borders, this is a wonderful pattern to show them off.

Difficulty Rating

Yarn

Stylecraft Classique Cotton (100% cotton), 3 light (8-ply/double knitting), 50g (101yd/92m), in the following shades:

> Plum (3567); 1 skein

> Wisteria (3664); 1 skein

Supplies

Size G (4mm) hook

Finished Size

$8^3/_4$ x $8^3/_4$in (22 x 22cm)

Gauge (Tension)

4 tiles measure just over $2^1/_2$in (6.25cm) using size G (4mm) hook and Stylecraft Classique Cotton

Stitch

Double crochet (UK treble crochet) C2C

NOTES

◢ *Divide the skein of darker colored yarn into two balls before beginning so that one can be attached on either side of the heart. Drop the lighter colored yarn toward the WS at each color change (do not cut) so that it's available to pick up on the next row.*

Instructions

TO MAKE THE WASHCLOTH

> Follow the written pattern and graph to crochet the washcloth. Do not fasten off Plum when finished.

> For borders, work as described below or experiment with your favorite decorative borders:

Border Round 1: Attach Wisteria to last C2C tile. Work one round of single crochet border (see General Techniques: Single Crochet Border). Fasten off.

Border Round 2: Pick up Plum. Ch 2 (counts as 1 hdc), 2 hdc in same sp, 3 hdc in each ch2sp, working 2 hdc in both sc sts at each corner, slst to first hdc to join. Fasten off. Weave in ends.

TIP

Make several of the heart blocks in different colours and seam them together for a child's blanket.

Pattern

◀ **Row 1 [RS]:** Plum x 1

▶ **Row 2 [WS]:** Plum x 2

◀ **Row 3:** Plum x 3

▶ **Row 4:** Plum x 4

◀ **Row 5:** Plum x 5

▶ **Row 6:** Plum x 6

◀ **Row 7:** Plum x 7

▶ **Row 8:** Plum x 8

◀ **Row 9:** Plum x 9

▶ **Row 10:** Plum x 3, Wisteria x 5, Plum x 2

◀ **Row 11:** Plum x 2, Wisteria x 5, Plum x 4

▶ **Row 12:** Plum x 4, Wisteria x 5, Plum x 3

◀ **Row 13:** Plum x 3, Wisteria x 5, Plum x 5

CORNER *(decrease at beginning of each row)*

▶ **Row 14 [WS]:** Plum x 4, Wisteria x 5, Plum x 3

◀ **Row 15 [RS]:** Plum x 5, Wisteria x 2, Plum x 4

▶ **Row 16:** Plum x 3, Wisteria x 3, Plum x 4

◀ **Row 17:** Plum x 4, Wisteria x 2, Plum x 3

▶ **Row 18:** Plum x 2, Wisteria x 3, Plum x 3

◀ **Row 19:** Plum x 3, Wisteria x 2, Plum x 2

▶ **Row 20:** Plum x 6

◀ **Row 21:** Plum x 5

▶ **Row 22:** Plum x 4

◀ **Row 23:** Plum x 3

▶ **Row 24:** Plum x 2

◀ **Row 25:** Plum x 1

LOVE SQUARED WASHCLOTH GRAPH

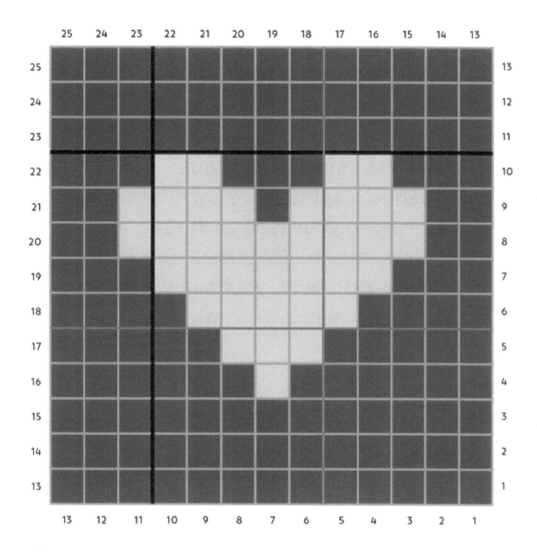

🟣 Stylecraft Classique Cotton – Plum

⚪ Stylecraft Classique Cotton – Wisteria

ON THE
PLUS SIDE RUG

Perk up your floors with this speedy rug pattern. The super-thick t-shirt style yarn makes this a quick gratification project with long-wearing results. Since each "plus" sign can be worked without cutting your yarn each row, you'll be left with very few ends to weave in. Try this pattern in different color combinations for a kid's bath, your spa sanctuary, or even a laundry room.

Difficulty Rating

Yarn

Lion Brand Fast-Track (60% cotton, 40% polyester blend), 6 super bulky (super chunky), 227g (149yd/136m), in the following shades:

› Dune Buggy Denim (108); 2 skeins

› Airstream White (100); 1 skein

Supplies

Size Q (15mm) hook

Smaller hook of approx. size K (6.5mm) to weave in ends

Finished Size

$25^{1}/_{4}$ x $17^{1}/_{2}$in (64 x 44.5cm)

Gauge (Tension)

4 tiles measure $4^{3}/_{4}$in (12cm) using size Q (15mm) hook and Lion Brand Fast-Track

Stitch

Double crochet (UK treble crochet) C2C

NOTES

◢ If you don't have access to a chunky, t-shirt style yarn, you can hold three to four strands of worsted weight cotton yarn together to create a similar long-wearing, absorbent yarn. If the rug size is important to you, check your gauge with the alternate yarn before you begin.

◢ Each "plus" sign requires roughly 17in (43cm) of White yarn. It can be helpful to wind off several 17in (43cm)/10g White bobbins and a handful of Denim bobbins in varying lengths to avoid cutting your *working yarn unnecessarily (see Managing Yarns: Tips For Wrangling Your Yarn).*

Instructions

TO MAKE THE RUG

› Follow the written pattern and graph to make the rug.

› For the borders, work as described below, using Denim:

Border Round 1: Work one round of single crochet border (see General Techniques: Single Crochet Border).

Border Round 2: Ch 3, *2 dc in next ch2sp, dc in next sc; repeat from * to beginning of round working 2 dc in both sc sts at each corner, slst to third ch from beginning of round to join. Fasten off.

Weave in ends.

TIP

You will likely find that using a smaller crochet hook to weave in ends is easier than using a tapestry needle with this particular yarn.

Pattern

◀ **Row 1 [RS]:** Denim x 1

▶ **Row 2 [WS]:** Denim x 2

◀ **Row 3:** Denim x 3

▶ **Row 4:** Denim x 4

◀ **Row 5:** Denim x 5

▶ **Row 6:** Denim x 2, White x 2, Denim x 2

◀ **Row 7:** Denim x 3, White x 1, Denim x 3

▶ **Row 8:** Denim x 3, White x 2, Denim x 3

◀ **Row 9:** Denim x 9

▶ **Row 10:** Denim x 10

◀ **Row 11:** Denim x 11

▶ **Row 12:** Denim x 2, White x 2, (Denim x 1, White x 2) twice, Denim x 2

◀ **Row 13:** Denim x 3, (White x 1, Denim x 2) twice, White x 1, Denim x 3

CORNER *(increase at beginning of WS rows, decrease at beginning of RS rows)*

▶ **Row 14 [WS]:** Denim x 3, (White x 2, Denim x 1) twice, White x 2, Denim x 2

◀ **Row 15 [RS]:** Denim x 13

▶ **Row 16:** Denim x 13

◀ **Row 17:** Denim x 13

▶ **Row 18:** Denim x 2, (White x 2, Denim x 1) twice, White x 2, Denim x 3

◀ **Row 19:** Denim x 3, (White x 1, Denim x 2) twice, White x 1, Denim x 3

CORNER *(decrease at beginning of each row)*

▶ **Row 20 [WS]:** Denim x 2, White x 2, (Denim x 1, White x 2) twice, Denim x 2

◀ **Row 21 [RS]:** Denim x 11

▶ **Row 22:** Denim x 10

◀ **Row 23:** Denim x 9

▶ **Row 24:** Denim x 3, White x 2, Denim x 3

◀ **Row 25:** Denim x 3, White x 1, Denim x 3

▶ **Row 26:** Denim x 2, White x 2, Denim x 2

◀ **Row 27:** Denim x 5

▶ **Row 28:** Denim x 4

◀ **Row 29:** Denim x 3

▶ **Row 30:** Denim x 2

◀ **Row 31:** Denim x 1

ON THE PLUS SIDE RUG GRAPH

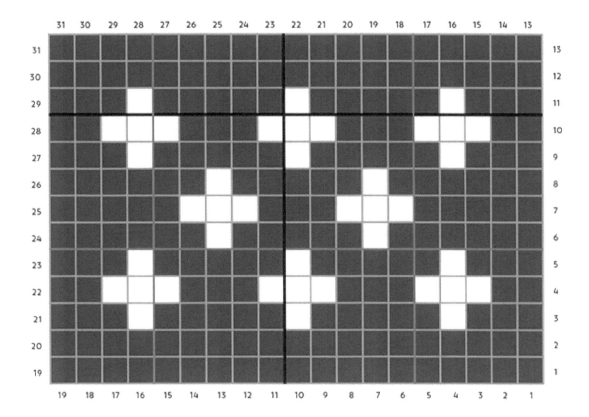

 Lion Brand Fast-Track – Dune Buggy Denim

Lion Brand Fast-Track – Airstream White

CRESTED BUTTE
COWL

Beginner doesn't have to be boring! This entry-level cowl makes an excellent first corner to corner project because it's nothing more than a rectangle – a mere 104 C2C tiles to be exact! Basic ribbing and oversized wooden buttons complete the look for a richly-textured and oh-so-squishy result.

Difficulty Rating

Yarn

Wool and The Gang Crazy Sexy Wool (100% wool), 6 super bulky (super chunky), 200g (87yd/80m), in the following shade:

› Cameo Rose (36); 2 skeins

Supplies

Size S (19mm) hook

4 x 1^1/$_2$in (4cm) buttons

Sewing thread to match buttons

Sewing needle

Finished Size

31 x 16in (78.75 x 40.75cm) with finished cowl laying flat

Gauge (Tension)

Main cowl: 4 tiles measure 8in (20cm) using size S (19mm) hook and Wool and The Gang Crazy Sexy Wool

Ribbing: 3 sc width measure 2^1/$_2$in (6.5cm) and 6 rows measure 4in (10cm) using size S (19mm) hook and Wool and The Gang Crazy Sexy Wool

Stitch

Double crochet (UK treble crochet) C2C

NOTES

▲ *If you'd like to substitute a yarn with a slightly different gauge for this simple cowl, just work a C2C rectangle until the dimensions are approximately 26 x 16in (66 x 40.75cm). Experiment with the number*

*of stitches and rows of a basic single crochet ribbing described below
to meet the approximate dimensions of 2^1/$_2$ x 16in (6 x 40.75cm).*

Instructions

TO MAKE THE COWL

› Follow the written pattern and graph to make main cowl piece.

› When finished, leave working yarn attached in corner.

› For borders, work as described below:

Using yarn still attached at corner, work single crochet border (see
General Techniques: Single Crochet Border) along long edge of cowl
only, fasten off leaving 30in (76cm) tail (note that the side facing
while working this row is now RS).

With RS facing, attach yarn at corner of second long edge. Work
single crochet border along long edge, fasten off leaving a 30in
(76cm) tail.

› For the ribbing, if you wish to have functioning buttonholes on your
cowl, work one of each of the two ribbing sections below. If you'd
prefer to avoid the buttonholes and just sew the buttons on for
aesthetics, make two non-buttonhole ribbing pieces.

› RIBBING WITHOUT BUTTONHOLES:

Foundation Row: Ch 4.

Row 1: Sk first sc, sc in each ch, turn. (3 sts)

Rows 2-28: Ch 1, sc in each sc, turn.

Fasten off.

› RIBBING WITH BUTTONHOLES:

Foundation Row: Ch 4.

Row 1: Sk first sc, sc in each ch, turn. (3 sts)

Rows 2-3: Ch 1, sc in each sc, turn.

Row 4: Ch 1, sc in first sc, ch 1, sk next sc, sc in last sc, turn
(buttonhole made).

Row 5: Ch 1, sc in each sc and ch1sp, turn. (3 sts)

Rows 6-10: Repeat Row 2.

Rows 11-24: Repeat Rows 4-10 twice.

Row 25: Repeat Row 4.

Rows 26-28: Repeat Row 2.

Fasten off.

> For finishing, lay long side of ribbing next to short side of cowl, WS facing up. Use the tails from the borders and the joining stitch to seam (see General Techniques: Joining C2C Pieces).

> Repeat on opposite side with second ribbing piece.

> Use a sewing needle and thread to attach buttons to non-buttonhole piece of ribbing.

> Weave in any remaining ends.

Pattern

◀ **Row 1 [RS]:** Rose x 1

▶ **Row 2 [WS]:** Rose x 2

◀ **Row 3:** Rose x 3

▶ **Row 4:** Rose x 4

◀ **Row 5:** Rose x 5

▶ **Row 6:** Rose x 6

◀ **Row 7:** Rose x 7

▶ **Row 8:** Rose x 8

CORNER *(increase at beginning of WS rows, decrease at beginning of RS rows)*

◀ **Row 9 [RS]:** Rose x 8

▶ **Row 10 [WS]:** Rose x 8

◀ **Row 11:** Rose x 8

▶ **Row 12:** Rose x 8

◀ **Row 13:** Rose x 8

CORNER *(decrease at beginning of each row)*

▶ **Row 14 [WS]:** Rose x 7

◀ **Row 15 [RS]:** Rose x 6

▶ **Row 16:** Rose x 5

◀ **Row 17:** Rose x 4

▶ **Row 18:** Rose x 3

◀ **Row 19:** Rose x 2

▶ **Row 20:** Rose x 1

CRESTED BUTTE COWL GRAPH

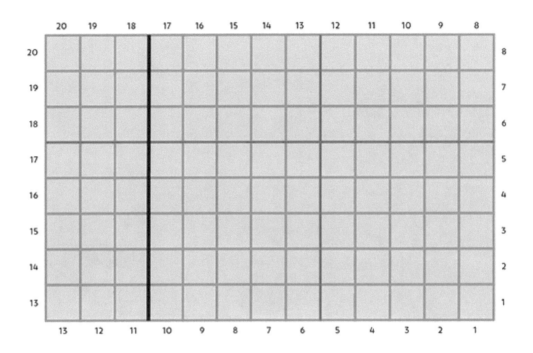

Wool and The Gang Crazy Sexy Wool – Cameo Rose

BRUSHSTROKES
SCARF

Time for triangles! Worked holding two strands of yarn together throughout, this simple scarf beautifully accentuates the gradual color changes in this yarn. While the sample was created with both skeins started at close to the same place in the color transitions, you may also experiment with aligning two different colors so as to create a more marled, higher contrast look.

Difficulty Rating

Yarn

Lion Brand Mandala (100% acrylic), 4 worsted (10-ply/aran), 150g (590yd/540m), in the following shade:

> Centaur (214); 3 skeins (scarf requires 2 skeins, tassels require 1 skein)

Supplies

Size K (6.5mm) hook

Tassel maker or $3\frac{1}{4}$in (8cm) piece of cardboard

Finished Size

53 x 26in (134.5 x 66cm) excluding tassels

Gauge (Tension)

4 tiles measure slightly over $3\frac{3}{4}$in (9.5cm) using size K (6.5mm) hook and Lion Brand Mandala

Stitch

Double crochet (UK treble crochet) C2C

NOTES

◢ This triangle is worked just like the first half of any C2C square. The final row fills in the "stair steps" of the raw C2C edge to create a smooth edge along the top of the scarf (see General Techniques: Finishing Off a Raw Edge).

◢ The sample was crocheted with two complete skeins. A portion of the third skein was used to create the tassels.

◢ If you desire a different size scarf than listed, simply work more or fewer rows of C2C.

◢ *This easy pattern can be worked in any self-striping yarn. Simply adjust your hook size accordingly (you want to find a hook that gives your scarf a decent "floppy" factor, but doesn't create such an open weave that the stitch definition is lost).*

Instructions

TO MAKE THE SCARF

› Follow the written pattern and graph to make the scarf.

› Reserve enough yarn for final border row described below, which is worked along "raw" edge of triangle (see General Techniques: Finishing Off a Raw Edge).

› For the border, work as described below:

Upper Edge Border (Row 39): Slst 4 along top edge of final C2C tile, [sc, hdc, dc] in ch-3 of same tile, *slst 1 in ch-3 of next tile, [sc, hdc, dc] in same tile; repeat from * until 1 tile remains.

Fasten off and weave in ends.

› To finish, using last skein of yarn and a tassel maker or piece of cardboard of size $3^1/4$in (8cm), make 17 tassels that roughly match the color transitions of scarf. Wrap yarn about 50 times to achieve tassel density pictured.

› Use a tapestry needle to attach tassels approximately 5in (12.75cm) apart along two shortest triangle sides (see General Techniques: Making a Tassel).

Pattern

◀ **Row 1 [RS]:** Centaur x 1

▶ **Row 2 [WS]:** Centaur x 2

◀ **Row 3:** Centaur x 3

▶ **Row 4:** Centaur x 4

◀ **Row 5:** Centaur x 5

▶ **Row 6:** Centaur x 6

◀ **Row 7:** Centaur x 7

▶ **Row 8:** Centaur x 8

◀ **Row 9:** Centaur x 9

▶ **Row 10:** Centaur x 10

◀ **Row 11:** Centaur x 11

▶ **Row 12:** Centaur x 12

◀ **Row 13:** Centaur x 13

▶ **Row 14:** Centaur x 14

◀ **Row 15:** Centaur x 15

▶ **Row 16:** Centaur x 16

◀ **Row 17:** Centaur x 17

▶ **Row 18:** Centaur x 18

◀ **Row 19:** Centaur x 19

▶ **Row 20:** Centaur x 20

◀ **Row 21:** Centaur x 21

▶ **Row 22:** Centaur x 22

◀ **Row 23:** Centaur x 23

▶ **Row 24:** Centaur x 24

◀ **Row 25:** Centaur x 25

▶ **Row 26:** Centaur x 26

◀ **Row 27:** Centaur x 27

▶ **Row 28:** Centaur x 28

◀ **Row 29:** Centaur x 29

▶ **Row 30:** Centaur x 30

◀ **Row 31:** Centaur x 31

▶ **Row 32:** Centaur x 32

◀ **Row 33:** Centaur x 33

▶ **Row 34:** Centaur x 34

◀ **Row 35:** Centaur x 35

▶ **Row 36:** Centaur x 36

◀ **Row 37:** Centaur x 37

▶ **Row 38:** Centaur x 38

BRUSHSTROKES SCARF GRAPH

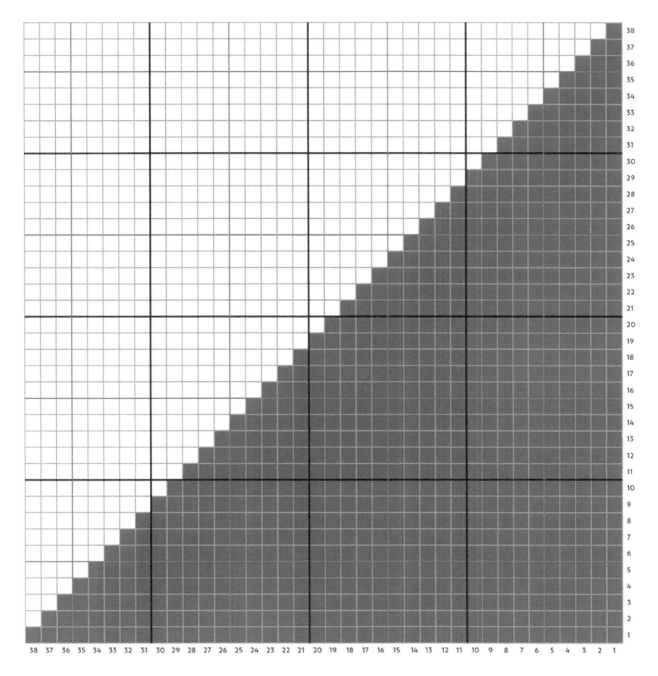

Lion Brand Mandala – Centaur

ENDLESS SKY
PONCHO

The illustrative character of C2C lends itself well to tribal-style geometric motifs. While this garment is made from basic rectangles, the graphically patterned fabric creates a surprisingly sophisticated-looking result. A palette of hues inspired by nature further imbue this piece with a warm earthy charm.

Difficulty Rating

Yarn

Quince & Co Owl (50% American wool, 50% alpaca), 4 worsted (10-ply/aran), 50g (120 yd/110m) in the following shades:

› Abyssinian; 8 (12-13) skeins

› Canyon; 1 (1) skein

› Cerulean; 1 (1) skein

› Cinnamon; 1 (2) skein(s)

› Huckleberry; 3 (4) skeins

Supplies

Size J (6mm) hook

Measurements and Sizing

Women's sizes: S/M (L/XL/2XL)

Fits bust: 34-40in/42-50in (86.25-101.5cm/107-127cm)

Finished measurements when laying flat: 33 x 26in/41 x 29^1/$_2$in (84 x 66cm/104 x 75cm)

Gauge (Tension)

Main poncho: 4 tiles measure 3^1/$_4$in (8.25cm) using size J (6mm) hook and Quince & Co Owl

Ribbing: 8 rows and 14 sts measure approx. 4in (10cm)

Stitch

Double crochet (UK treble crochet) C2C

NOTES

◢ Pattern is worked in three main pieces and seamed. Ribbing is worked separately and seamed to main garment.

◢ Just when you think you have too many colors to manage at one time in this pattern, you'll fasten them off and work a stretch of solid color. See Managing Your Yarns: *Tips For Wrangling Your Yarn* for bobbin management ideas to help organize your yarn as you work.

◢ To create a longer garment, add the same number of extra solid color rows in the middle of each piece (note that this will make your project different than the written instructions below, but the general number of tiles for each stretch of color will remain the same).

Instructions

TO MAKE THE PONCHO

› Follow the written pattern and graphs to make one back piece, one left front and one right front for size desired.

› It is more important that your ribbing fits the piece it will be attached to, rather than achieving the specific number of rows stated. You can increase or decrease the number of rows as necessary.

› For ribbing, use Huckleberry and work as follows:

› **BACK RIBBING (MAKE 1):**

Foundation Row: Ch 20.

Row 1 : Sk 2 ch, hdc in each ch to end of row, turn. (18 sts)

Rows 2-68 (82): Ch 2, hdc in the back loop of each hdc, turn.

Piece should have 34 (41) bumps of ribbing. Fasten off leaving a 36in (91.5cm) tail.

› **FRONT RIBBING (MAKE 2):**

Foundation Row: Ch 20.

Row 1: Sk 2 ch, hdc in each ch to end of row, turn. (18 sts)

Rows 2-24 (30): Ch 2, hdc in the back loop of each hdc, turn.

Piece should have 12 (15) bumps of ribbing. Fasten off leaving a 24in (61cm) tail.

› COLLAR RIBBING (MAKE 1):

Foundation Row: Ch 10.

Row 1: Sk 2 ch, hdc in each ch to end of row, turn. (8 sts)

Rows 2-125 (139): Ch 2, hdc in the back loop of each hdc, turn.

Piece should have 62 (69) bumps of ribbing. Fasten off leaving a 36in (91.5cm) tail.

› For joining, first block pieces if desired. Complete all seaming with a tapestry needle, Abyssinian yarn and the stitch described in Joining C2C Pieces (see General Techniques) unless otherwise noted.

› With pieces next to each other and RS facing down, pin back ribbing to bottom of back piece. Seam and fasten off yarn. Repeat same process to seam front ribbing and both front pieces.

› With RS facing down, pin back and two front pieces at shoulders. Seam from outer shoulder along shoulder edge. Fasten off when neck is reached. Repeat with second shoulder.

› On each side edge, place pin right above bottom ribbing as well as $8^1/_2$-10in (21.5-25cm) up from bottom edge. Seam length between pins on both right and left side of garment.

› With RS facing, pin collar ribbing along edge of front piece, along the back of the neck and down the edge of the second front piece. Seam and fasten off.

› Weave in remaining ends.

Pattern

LEFT FRONT (ALL SIZES)

◀ **Row 1 [RS]:** Abyssinian x 1

▶ **Row 2 [WS]:** Huckleberry x 1, Abyssinian x 1

◀ **Row 3:** Cinnamon x 1, Abyssinian x 1, Huckleberry x 1

▶ **Row 4:** Cerulean x 1, Huckleberry x 1, Abyssinian x 1, Cinnamon x 1

◀ **Row 5 :** Canyon x 1, Cinnamon x 1, Abyssinian x 1, Huckleberry x 1, Cerulean x 1

▶ **Row 6:** Cerulean x 2, Huckleberry x 1, Abyssinian x 1, Cinnamon x 2

◀ **Row 7:** Cinnamon x 3, Abyssinian x 1, Huckleberry x 3

▶ **Row 8:** Huckleberry x 4, Abyssinian x 4

◀ **Row 9:** Abyssinian x 9

▶ **Row 10:** Abyssinian x 5, Huckleberry x 4, Abyssinian x 1

◀ **Row 11:** Abyssinian x 2, Huckleberry x 3, Abyssinian x 1, Cinnamon x 4, Abyssinian x 1

▶ **Row 12:** Huckleberry x 1, Abyssinian x 1, Cinnamon x 3, Abyssinian x 1, Huckleberry x 1, Cerulean x 2, Abyssinian x 3

◀ **Row 13:** Abyssinian x 4, Cerulean x 1, Huckleberry x 1, Abyssinian x 1, Cinnamon x 1, Canyon x 2, Cinnamon x 1, Abyssinian x 1, Huckleberry x 1

▶ **Row 14:** Cerulean x 1, Huckleberry x 1, Abyssinian x 1, Cinnamon x 1, Canyon x 1, Cinnamon x 1, Abyssinian x 1, Huckleberry x 1, Cerulean x 1, Abyssinian x 5

◀ **Row 15:** Abyssinian x 6, Huckleberry x 1, Abyssinian x 1, Cinnamon x 1, Canyon x 2, Cinnamon x 1, Abyssinian x 1, Huckleberry x 1, Cerulean x 1

▶ **Row 16:** Cerulean x 2, Huckleberry x 1, Abyssinian x 1, Cinnamon x 3, Abyssinian x 1, Huckleberry x 1, Abyssinian x 7

Proceed with instructions for specific size below:

LEFT FRONT (S/M), CONT.

CORNER *(increase at beginning of RS rows, decrease at beginning of WS rows)*

◀ **Row 17 [RS]:** Abyssinian x 9, Cinnamon x 4, Abyssinian x 1, Huckleberry x 2

▶ **Row 18 [WS]:** Huckleberry x 2, Abyssinian x 14

◀ **Row 19:** Abyssinian x 16

▶ **Row 20:** Abyssinian x 1, Huckleberry x 4, Abyssinian x 11

◀ **Row 21:** Abyssinian x 12, Huckleberry x 3, Abyssinian x 1

▶ **Row 22:** Huckleberry x 1, Cerulean x 2, Abyssinian x 13

◀ **Row 23:** Abyssinian x 14, Cerulean x 1, Huckleberry x 1

▶ **Row 24:** Cerulean x 1, Abyssinian x 15

◀ **Row 25:** Abyssinian x 16

▶ **Row 26:** Abyssinian x 16

◀ **Row 27:** Abyssinian x 16

▶ **Row 28:** Abyssinian x 15, Cerulean x 1

◀ **Row 29:** Cerulean x 1, Huckleberry x 1, Abyssinian x 14

CORNER *(decrease at beginning of each row)*

▶ **Row 30 [WS]:** Abyssinian x 13, Huckleberry x 1, Cerulean x 1

◀ **Row 31 [RS]:** Huckleberry x 1, Cerulean x 1, Abyssinian x 12

▶ **Row 32:** Abyssinian x 11, Cerulean x 1, Huckleberry x 1

◀ **Row 33:** Cerulean x 1, Cinnamon x 1, Abyssinian x 10

▶ **Row 34:** Abyssinian x 9, Cinnamon x 1, Cerulean x 1

◀ **Row 35:** Cinnamon x 1, Canyon x 1, Abyssinian x 8

▶ **Row 36:** Abyssinian x 7, Canyon x 1, Cinnamon x 1

◀ **Row 37:** Canyon x 1, Cinnamon x 1, Abyssinian x 6

▶ **Row 38:** Abyssinian x 5, Cinnamon x 1, Canyon x 1

◀ **Row 39:** Cinnamon x 1, Cerulean x 1, Abyssinian x 4

▶ **Row 40:** Abyssinian x 3, Cerulean x 1, Cinnamon x 1

◀ **Row 41:** Cerulean x 1, Huckleberry x 1, Abyssinian x 2

▶ **Row 42:** Abyssinian x 1, Huckleberry x 1, Cerulean x 1

◀ **Row 43:** Huckleberry x 1, Cerulean x 1

▶ **Row 44:** Huckleberry x 1

LEFT FRONT (L/XL/2XL), CONT.

◀ **Row 17 [RS]:** Abyssinian x 9, Cinnamon x 4, Abyssinian x 1, Huckleberry x 3

▶ **Row 18 [WS]:** Huckleberry x 4, Abyssinian x 14

◀ **Row 19:** Abyssinian x 19

▶ **Row 20:** Abyssinian x 5, Huckleberry x 4, Abyssinian x 11

CORNER *(increase at beginning of rs rows, decrease at beginning of ws rows)*

◀ **Row 21 [RS]:** Abyssinian x 12, Huckleberry x 3, Abyssinian x 1, Cinnamon x 4

▶ **Row 22 [WS]:** Cinnamon x 3, Abyssinian x 1, Huckleberry x 1, Cerulean x 2, Abyssinian x 13

◀ **Row 23:** Abyssinian x 14, Cerulean x 1, Huckleberry x 1, Abyssinian x 1, Cinnamon x 1, Canyon x 2

▶ **Row 24:** Canyon x 1, Cinnamon x 1, Abyssinian x 1, Huckleberry x 1, Cerulean x 1, Abyssinian x 15

◀ **Row 25:** Abyssinian x 16, Huckleberry x 1, Abyssinian x 1, Cinnamon x 1, Canyon x 1

▶ **Row 26 :** Cinnamon x 1, Abyssinian x 1, Huckleberry x 1, Abyssinian x 17

◀ **Row 27:** Abyssinian x 19, Cinnamon x 1

▶ **Row 28:** Abyssinian x 20

◀ **Row 29 :** Abyssinian x 20

▶ **Row 30:** Abyssinian x 20

◀ **Row 31:** Abyssinian x 20

▶ **Row 32:** Abyssinian x 19, Canyon x 1

◀ **Row 33:** Canyon x 1, Cinnamon x 1, Abyssinian x 18

CORNER *(decrease at beginning of each row)*

▶ **Row 34 [WS]:** Abyssinian x 17, Cinnamon x 1, Canyon x 1

◀ **Row 35 [RS]:** Cinnamon x 1, Cerulean x 1, Abyssinian x 16

▶ **Row 36:** Abyssinian x 15, Cerulean x 1, Cinnamon x 1

◀ **Row 37:** Cerulean x 1, Huckleberry x 1, Abyssinian x 14

▶ **Row 38:** Abyssinian x 13, Huckleberry x 1, Cerulean x 1

◀ **Row 39:** Huckleberry x 1, Cerulean x 1, Abyssinian x 12

▶ **Row 40:** Abyssinian x 11, Cerulean x 1, Huckleberry x 1

◀ **Row 41:** Cerulean x 1, Cinnamon x 1, Abyssinian x 10

▶ **Row 42:** Abyssinian x 9, Cinnamon x 1, Cerulean x 1

◀ **Row 43:** Cinnamon x 1, Canyon x 1, Abyssinian x 8

▶ **Row 44:** Abyssinian x 7, Canyon x 1, Cinnamon x 1

◀ **Row 45:** Canyon x 1, Cinnamon x 1, Abyssinian x 6

▶ **Row 46:** Abyssinian x 5, Cinnamon x 1, Canyon x 1

◀ **Row 47:** Cinnamon x 1, Cerulean x 1, Abyssinian x 4

▶ **Row 48:** Abyssinian x 3, Cerulean x 1, Cinnamon x 1

◀ **Row 49:** Cerulean x 1, Huckleberry x 1, Abyssinian x 2

▶ **Row 50:** Abyssinian x 1, Huckleberry x 1, Cerulean x 1

◀ **Row 51:** Huckleberry x 1, Cerulean x 1

▶ **Row 52:** Huckleberry x 1

RIGHT FRONT (S/M)

◀ **Row 1 [RS]:** Cerulean x 1

▶ **Row 2 [WS]:** Cerulean x 1, Huckleberry x 1

◀ **Row 3:** Huckleberry x 1, Cerulean x 2

▶ **Row 4:** Huckleberry x 3, Abyssinian x 1

◀ **Row 5:** Abyssinian x 1, Huckleberry x 4

▶ **Row 6:** Abyssinian x 6

◀ **Row 7:** Huckleberry x 2, Abyssinian x 5

▶ **Row 8:** Abyssinian x 1, Cinnamon x 4, Abyssinian x 1, Huckleberry x 2

◀ **Row 9:** Cerulean x 2, Huckleberry x 1, Abyssinian x 1, Cinnamon x 3, Abyssinian x 1, Huckleberry x 1

▶ **Row 10:** Huckleberry x 1, Abyssinian x 1, Cinnamon x 1, Canyon x 2, Cinnamon x 1, Abyssinian x 1, Huckleberry x 1, Cerulean x 1,

Abyssinian x 1

◀ **Row 11:** Abyssinian x 2, Cerulean x 1, Huckleberry x 1, Abyssinian x 1, Cinnamon x 1, Canyon x 1, Cinnamon x 1, Abyssinian x 1, Huckleberry x 1, Cerulean x 1

▶ **Row 12:** Cerulean x 1, Huckleberry x 1, Abyssinian x 1, Cinnamon x 1, Canyon x 2, Cinnamon x 1, Abyssinian x 1, Huckleberry x 1, Abyssinian x 3

◀ **Row 13:** Abyssinian x 4, Huckleberry x 1, Abyssinian x 1, Cinnamon x 3, Abyssinian x 1, Huckleberry x 1, Cerulean x 2

▶ **Row 14:** Huckleberry x 3, Abyssinian x 1, Cinnamon x 4, Abyssinian x 6

◀ **Row 15:** Abyssinian x 11, Huckleberry x 4

▶ **Row 16:** Abyssinian x 16

CORNER *(increase at beginning of RS rows, decrease at beginning of WS rows)*

◀ **Row 17 [RS]:** Abyssinian x 8, Huckleberry x 4, Abyssinian x 4

▶ **Row 18 [WS]:** Cinnamon x 3, Abyssinian x 1, Huckleberry x 3, Abyssinian x 9

◀ **Row 19:** Abyssinian x 10, Cerulean x 2, Huckleberry x 1, Abyssinian x 1, Cinnamon x 2

▶ **Row 20:** Canyon x 1, Cinnamon x 1, Abyssinian x 1, Huckleberry x 1, Cerulean x 1, Abyssinian x 11

◀ **Row 21:** Abyssinian x 12, Cerulean x 1, Huckleberry x 1, Abyssinian x 1, Cinnamon x 1

▶ **Row 22:** Cinnamon x 1, Abyssinian x 1, Huckleberry x 1, Abyssinian x 13

◀ **Row 23:** Abyssinian x 14, Huckleberry x 1, Abyssinian x 1

▶ **Row 24:** Abyssinian x 16

◀ **Row 25:** Abyssinian x 16

▶ **Row 26:** Abyssinian x 16

◀ **Row 27:** Abyssinian x 16

▶ **Row 28:** Abyssinian x 15, Cerulean x 1

◀ **Row 29:** Huckleberry x 2, Abyssinian x 14

CORNER *(decrease at beginning of each row)*

▶ **Row 30 [WS]:** Abyssinian x 13, Huckleberry x 2

◀ **Row 31 [RS]:** Cerulean x 2, Abyssinian x 12

▶ **Row 32:** Abyssinian x 11, Cerulean x 2

◀ **Row 33:** Cinnamon x 2, Abyssinian x 10

▶ **Row 34:** Abyssinian x 9, Cinnamon x 2

◀ **Row 35:** Canyon x 2, Abyssinian x 8

▶ **Row 36:** Abyssinian x 7, Canyon x 2

◀ **Row 37:** Cinnamon x 2, Abyssinian x 6

▶ **Row 38:** Abyssinian x 5, Cinnamon x 2

◀ **Row 39:** Cerulean x 2, Abyssinian x 4

▶ **Row 40:** Abyssinian x 3, Cerulean x 2

◀ **Row 41:** Huckleberry x 2, Abyssinian x 2

▶ **Row 42:** Abyssinian x 1, Huckleberry x 2

◀ **Row 43:** Cerulean x 2

▶ **Row 44:** Cerulean x 1

RIGHT FRONT (L/XL/2XL)

◀ **Row 1 [RS]:** Abyssinian x 1

▶ **Row 2 [WS]:** Abyssinian x 1, Cinnamon x 1

◀ **Row 3:** Cinnamon x 1, Abyssinian x 1, Huckleberry x 1

▶ **Row 4:** Huckleberry x 1, Abyssinian x 1, Cinnamon x 1, Canyon x 1

◀ **Row 5:** Canyon x 1, Cinnamon x 1, Abyssinian x 1, Huckleberry x 1, Cerulean x 1

▶ **Row 6:** Cerulean x 1, Huckleberry x 1, Abyssinian x 1, Cinnamon x 1, Canyon x 2

◀ **Row 7:** Cinnamon x 3, Abyssinian x 1, Huckleberry x 1, Cerulean x 2

▶ **Row 8:** Huckleberry x 3, Abyssinian x 1, Cinnamon x 4

◄ **Row 9:** Abyssinian x 5, Huckleberry x 4

► **Row 10:** Abyssinian x 10

◄ **Row 11:** Abyssinian x 2, Huckleberry x 4, Abyssinian x 5

► **Row 12:** Abyssinian x 1, Cinnamon x 4, Abyssinian x 1, Huckleberry x 3, Abyssinian x 3

◄ **Row 13:** Abyssinian x 4, Cerulean x 2, Huckleberry x 1, Abyssinian x 1, Cinnamon x 3, Abyssinian x 1, Huckleberry x 1

► **Row 14:** Huckleberry x 1, Abyssinian x 1, Cinnamon x 1, Canyon x 2, Cinnamon x 1, Abyssinian x 1, Huckleberry x 1, Cerulean x 1, Abyssinian x 5

◄ **Row 15:** Abyssinian x 6, Cerulean x 1, Huckleberry x 1, Abyssinian x 1, Cinnamon x 1, Canyon x 1, Cinnamon x 1, Abyssinian x 1, Huckleberry x 1, Cerulean x 1

► **Row 16:** Cerulean x 1, Huckleberry x 1, Abyssinian x 1, Cinnamon x 1, Canyon x 2, Cinnamon x 1, Abyssinian x 1, Huckleberry x 1, Abyssinian x 7

◄ **Row 17:** Abyssinian x 8, Huckleberry x 1, Abyssinian x 1, Cinnamon x 3, Abyssinian x 1, Huckleberry x 1, Cerulean x 2

► **Row 18:** Huckleberry x 3, Abyssinian x 1, Cinnamon x 4, Abyssinian x 10

◄ **Row 19:** Abyssinian x 15, Huckleberry x 4

► **Row 20:** Abyssinian x 20

CORNER *(increase at beginning of RS rows, decrease at beginning of WS rows)*

◄ **Row 21 [RS]:** Abyssinian x 12, Huckleberry x 4, Abyssinian x 4

► **Row 22 [WS]:** Cinnamon x 3, Abyssinian x 1, Huckleberry x 3, Abyssinian x 13

◄ **Row 23:** Abyssinian x 14, Cerulean x 2, Huckleberry x 1, Abyssinian x 1, Cinnamon x 2

► **Row 24:** Canyon x 1, Cinnamon x 1, Abyssinian x 1, Huckleberry x 1, Cerulean x 1, Abyssinian x 15

◄ **Row 25:** Abyssinian x 16, Cerulean x 1, Huckleberry x 1, Abyssinian x 1, Cinnamon x 1

▶ **Row 26:** Cinnamon x 1, Abyssinian x 1, Huckleberry x 1, Abyssinian x 17

◀ **Row 27:** Abyssinian x 18, Huckleberry x 1, Abyssinian x 1

▶ **Row 28:** Abyssinian x 20

◀ **Row 29:** Abyssinian x 20

▶ **Row 30:** Abyssinian x 20

◀ **Row 31:** Abyssinian x 20

▶ **Row 32:** Abyssinian x 19, Cerulean x 1

◀ **Row 33:** Huckleberry x 2, Abyssinian x 18

CORNER *(decrease at beginning of all rows)*

▶ **Row 34 [WS]:** Abyssinian x 17, Huckleberry x 2

◀ **Row 35 [RS]:** Cerulean x 2, Abyssinian x 16

▶ **Row 36:** Abyssinian x 15, Cerulean x 2

◀ **Row 37:** Cinnamon x 2, Abyssinian x 14

▶ **Row 38:** Abyssinian x 13, Cinnamon x 2

◀ **Row 39:** Canyon x 2, Abyssinian x 12

▶ **Row 40:** Abyssinian x 11, Canyon x 2

◀ **Row 41:** Cinnamon x 2, Abyssinian x 10

▶ **Row 42:** Abyssinian x 9, Cinnamon x 2

◀ **Row 43:** Cerulean x 2, Abyssinian x 8

▶ **Row 44:** Abyssinian x 7, Cerulean x 2

◀ **Row 45:** Huckleberry x 2, Abyssinian x 6

▶ **Row 46:** Abyssinian x 5, Huckleberry x 2

◀ **Row 47:** Cerulean x 2, Abyssinian x 4

▶ **Row 48:** Abyssinian x 3, Cerulean x 2

◀ **Row 49:** Cinnamon x 2, Abyssinian x 2

▶ **Row 50:** Abyssinian x 1, Cinnamon x 2

◀ **Row 51:** Canyon x 2

▶ **Row 52:** Canyon x 1

BACK (ALL SIZES)

◀ **Row 1 [RS]:** Abyssinian x 1

▶ **Row 2 [WS]:** Abyssinian x 1, Cinnamon x 1

◀ **Row 3:** Cinnamon x 1, Abyssinian x 1, Huckleberry x 1

▶ **Row 4:** Huckleberry x 1, Abyssinian x 1, Cinnamon x 1, Canyon x 1

◀ **Row 5:** Canyon x 1, Cinnamon x 1, Abyssinian x 1, Huckleberry x 1, Cerulean x 1

▶ **Row 6:** Cerulean x 1, Huckleberry x 1, Abyssinian x 1, Cinnamon x 1, Canyon x 2

◀ **Row 7:** Cinnamon x 3, Abyssinian x 1, Huckleberry x 1, Cerulean x 2

▶ **Row 8:** Huckleberry x 3, Abyssinian x 1, Cinnamon x 4

◀ **Row 9:** Abyssinian x 5, Huckleberry x 4

▶ **Row 10:** Abyssinian x 10

◀ **Row 11:** Abyssinian x 2, Huckleberry x 4, Abyssinian x 5

▶ **Row 12:** Abyssinian x 1, Cinnamon x 4, Abyssinian x 1, Huckleberry x 3, Abyssinian x 3

◀ **Row 13:** Abyssinian x 4, Cerulean x 2, Huckleberry x 1, Abyssinian x 1, Cinnamon x 3, Abyssinian x 1, Huckleberry x 1

▶ **Row 14:** Huckleberry x 1, Abyssinian x 1, Cinnamon x 1, Canyon x 2, Cinnamon x 1, Abyssinian x 1, Huckleberry x 1, Cerulean x 1, Abyssinian x 5

◀ **Row 15:** Abyssinian x 6, Cerulean x 1, Huckleberry x 1, Abyssinian x 1, Cinnamon x 1, Canyon x 1, Cinnamon x 1, Abyssinian x 1, Huckleberry x 1, Cerulean x 1

▶ **Row 16:** Cerulean x 1, Huckleberry x 1, Abyssinian x 1, Cinnamon x 1, Canyon x 2, Cinnamon x 1, Abyssinian x 1, Huckleberry x 1, Abyssinian x 7

◀ **Row 17:** Abyssinian x 8, Huckleberry x 1, Abyssinian x 1, Cinnamon x 3, Abyssinian x 1, Huckleberry x 1, Cerulean x 2

▶ **Row 18:** Huckleberry x 3, Abyssinian x 1, Cinnamon x 4, Abyssinian x 10

◀ **Row 19:** Abyssinian x 15, Huckleberry x 4

▶ **Row 20:** Abyssinian x 20

◀ **Row 21:** Abyssinian x 12, Huckleberry x 4, Abyssinian x 5

▶ **Row 22:** Abyssinian x 1, Cinnamon x 4, Abyssinian x 1, Huckleberry x 3, Abyssinian x 13

◀ **Row 23:** Abyssinian x 14, Cerulean x 2, Huckleberry x 1, Abyssinian x 1, Cinnamon x 3, Abyssinian x 1, Huckleberry x 1

▶ **Row 24:** Huckleberry x 1, Abyssinian x 1, Cinnamon x 1, Canyon x 2, Cinnamon x 1, Abyssinian x 1, Huckleberry x 1, Cerulean x 1, Abyssinian x 15

◀ **Row 25:** Abyssinian x 16, Cerulean x 1, Huckleberry x 1, Abyssinian x 1, Cinnamon x 1, Canyon x 1, Cinnamon x 1, Abyssinian x 1, Huckleberry x 1, Cerulean x 1

▶ **Row 26:** Cerulean x 1, Huckleberry x 1, Abyssinian x 1, Cinnamon x 1, Canyon x 2, Cinnamon x 1, Abyssinian x 1, Huckleberry x 1, Abyssinian x 17

◀ **Row 27:** Abyssinian x 18, Huckleberry x 1, Abyssinian x 1, Cinnamon x 3, Abyssinian x 1, Huckleberry x 1, Cerulean x 2

Proceed with instructions for specific size below:

BACK (S/M), CONT:

◀ **Row 28 [WS]:** Huckleberry x 3, Abyssinian x 1, Cinnamon x 4, Abyssinian x 19, Canyon x 1

▶ **Row 29 [RS]:** Cinnamon x 1, Canyon x 1, Abyssinian x 23, Huckleberry x 4

CORNER *(increase at beginning of rs rows, decrease at beginning of ws rows)*

▶ **Row 30 [WS]:** Abyssinian x 27, Cinnamon x 1, Canyon x 1

◀ **Row 31 [RS]:** Canyon x 1, Cinnamon x 1, Abyssinian x 18, Huckleberry x 4, Abyssinian x 5

▶ **Row 32:** Abyssinian x 1, Cinnamon x 4, Abyssinian x 1, Huckleberry x 3, Abyssinian x 18, Cerulean x 1, Cinnamon x 1

◀ **Row 33:** Cinnamon x 1, Cerulean x 1, Abyssinian x 18, Cerulean x 2, Huckleberry x 1, Abyssinian x 1, Cinnamon x 3, Abyssinian x 1, Huckleberry x 1

▶ **Row 34:** Huckleberry x 1, Abyssinian x 1, Cinnamon x 1, Canyon x 2, Cinnamon x 1, Abyssinian x 1, Huckleberry x 1, Cerulean x 1, Abyssinian x 18, Huckleberry x 1, Cerulean x 1

◀ **Row 35:** Cerulean x 1, Huckleberry x 1, Abyssinian x 18, Cerulean x 1, Huckleberry x 1, Abyssinian x 1, Cinnamon x 1, Canyon x 1, Cinnamon x 1, Abyssinian x 1, Huckleberry x 1, Cerulean x 1

▶ **Row 36:** Cerulean x 1, Huckleberry x 1, Abyssinian x 1, Cinnamon x 1, Canyon x 2, Cinnamon x 1, Abyssinian x 1, Huckleberry x 1, Abyssinian x 18, Cerulean x 1, Huckleberry x 1

◀ **Row 37:** Huckleberry x 1, Cerulean x 1, Abyssinian x 18, Huckleberry x 1, Abyssinian x 1, Cinnamon x 3, Abyssinian x 1, Huckleberry x 1, Cerulean x 2

▶ **Row 38:** Huckleberry x 3, Abyssinian x 1, Cinnamon x 4, Abyssinian x 19, Cinnamon x 1, Cerulean x 1

◀ **Row 39:** Cerulean x 1, Cinnamon x 1, Abyssinian x 23, Huckleberry x 4

▶ **Row 40:** Abyssinian x 27, Canyon x 1, Cinnamon x 1

◀ **Row 41:** Cinnamon x 1, Canyon x 1, Abyssinian x 18, Huckleberry x 4, Abyssinian x 5

CORNER *(decrease at beginning of each row)*

▶ **Row 42 [WS]:** Cinnamon x 4, Abyssinian x 1, Huckleberry x 3, Abyssinian x 18, Cinnamon x 1, Canyon x 1

◀ **Row 43 [RS]:** Canyon x 1, Cinnamon x 1, Abyssinian x 18, Cerulean x 2, Huckleberry x 1, Abyssinian x 1, Cinnamon x 3

▶ **Row 44:** Canyon x 2, Cinnamon x 1, Abyssinian x 1, Huckleberry x 1, Cerulean x 1, Abyssinian x 18, Cerulean x 1, Cinnamon x 1

◀ **Row 45:** Cinnamon x 1, Cerulean x 1, Abyssinian x 18, Cerulean x 1, Huckleberry x 1, Abyssinian x 1, Cinnamon x 1, Canyon x 1

▶ **Row 46:** Canyon x 1, Cinnamon x 1, Abyssinian x 1, Huckleberry x 1, Abyssinian x 18, Huckleberry x 1, Cerulean x 1

◀ **Row 47:** Cerulean x 1, Huckleberry x 1, Abyssinian x 18, Huckleberry x 1, Abyssinian x 1, Cinnamon x 1

▶ **Row 48:** Cinnamon x 1, Abyssinian x 19, Huckleberry x 2

◀ **Row 49:** Huckleberry x 2, Abyssinian x 19

▶ **Row 50:** Abyssinian x 18, Huckleberry x 2

◀ **Row 51:** Cerulean x 2, Abyssinian x 17

▶ **Row 52:** Abyssinian x 16, Cerulean x 2

◀ **Row 53:** Cinnamon x 2, Abyssinian x 15

▶ **Row 54:** Abyssinian x 14, Cinnamon x 2

◀ **Row 55:** Canyon x 2, Abyssinian x 13

▶ **Row 56:** Abyssinian x 12, Canyon x 2

◀ **Row 57:** Cinnamon x 2, Abyssinian x 11

▶ **Row 58:** Abyssinian x 10, Cinnamon x 2

◀ **Row 59:** Cerulean x 2, Abyssinian x 9

▶ **Row 60:** Abyssinian x 8, Cerulean x 2

◀ **Row 61:** Huckleberry x 2, Abyssinian x 7

▶ **Row 62:** Abyssinian x 6, Huckleberry x 2

◀ **Row 63:** Cerulean x 2, Abyssinian x 5

▶ **Row 64:** Abyssinian x 4, Cerulean x 2

◀ **Row 65:** Cinnamon x 2, Abyssinian x 3

▶ **Row 66:** Abyssinian x 2, Cinnamon x 2

◀ **Row 67:** Canyon x 2, Abyssinian x 1

▶ **Row 68:** Canyon x 2

◀ **Row 69:** Cinnamon x 1

BACK (L/XL/2XL), CONT.

▶ **Row 28 [WS]:** Huckleberry x 3, Abyssinian x 1, Cinnamon x 4, Abyssinian x 20

◀ **Row 29 [RS]:** Abyssinian x 25, Huckleberry x 4

▶ **Row 30:** Abyssinian x 30

◀ **Row 31:** Abyssinian x 22, Huckleberry x 4, Abyssinian x 5

▶ **Row 32:** Abyssinian x 1, Cinnamon x 4, Abyssinian x 1, Huckleberry x 3, Abyssinian x 22, Huckleberry x 1

◀ **Row 33:** Huckleberry x 1, Cerulean x 1, Abyssinian x 22, Cerulean x 2, Huckleberry x 1, Abyssinian x 1, Cinnamon x 3, Abyssinian x 1,

Huckleberry x 1

CORNER *(increase at beginning of rs rows, decrease at beginning of ws rows)*

▶ **Row 34 [WS]:** Huckleberry x 1, Abyssinian x 1, Cinnamon x 1, Canyon x 2, Cinnamon x 1, Abyssinian x 1, Huckleberry x 1, Cerulean x 1, Abyssinian x 22, Cerulean x 1, Huckleberry x 1

◀ **Row 35 [RS]:** Cerulean x 1, Cinnamon x 1, Abyssinian x 22, Cerulean x 1, Huckleberry x 1, Abyssinian x 1, Cinnamon x 1, Canyon x 1, Cinnamon x 1, Abyssinian x 1, Huckleberry x 1, Cerulean x 1

▶ **Row 36:** Cerulean x 1, Huckleberry x 1, Abyssinian x 1, Cinnamon x 1, Canyon x 2, Cinnamon x 1, Abyssinian x 1, Huckleberry x 1, Abyssinian x 22, Cinnamon x 1, Cerulean x 1

◀ **Row 37:** Cinnamon x 1, Canyon x 1, Abyssinian x 22, Huckleberry x 1, Abyssinian x 1, Cinnamon x 3, Abyssinian x 1, Huckleberry x 1, Cerulean x 2

▶ **Row 38:** Huckleberry x 3, Abyssinian x 1, Cinnamon x 4, Abyssinian x 23, Canyon x 1, Cinnamon x 1

◀ **Row 39:** Canyon x 1, Cinnamon x 1, Abyssinian x 27, Huckleberry x 4

▶ **Row 40:** Abyssinian x 31, Cinnamon x 1, Canyon x 1

◀ **Row 41:** Cinnamon x 1, Cerulean x 1, Abyssinian x 22, Huckleberry x 4, Abyssinian x 5

▶ **Row 42:** Abyssinian x 1, Cinnamon x 4, Abyssinian x 1, Huckleberry x 3, Abyssinian x 22, Cerulean x 1, Cinnamon x 1

◀ **Row 43:** Cerulean x 1, Huckleberry x 1, Abyssinian x 22, Cerulean x 2, Huckleberry x 1, Abyssinian x 1, Cinnamon x 3, Abyssinian x 1, Huckleberry x 1

▶ **Row 44:** Huckleberry x 1, Abyssinian x 1, Cinnamon x 1, Canyon x 2, Cinnamon x 1, Abyssinian x 1, Huckleberry x 1, Cerulean x 1, Abyssinian x 22, Huckleberry x 1, Cerulean x 1

◀ **Row 45:** Huckleberry x 1, Cerulean x 1, Abyssinian x 22, Cerulean x 1, Huckleberry x 1, Abyssinian x 1, Cinnamon x 1, Canyon x 1, Cinnamon x 1, Abyssinian x 1, Huckleberry x 1, Cerulean x 1

▶ **Row 46:** Cerulean x 1, Huckleberry x 1, Abyssinian x 1, Cinnamon x 1, Canyon x 2, Cinnamon x 1, Abyssinian x 1, Huckleberry x 1,

Abyssinian x 22, Cerulean x 1, Huckleberry x 1

◀ Row 47: Cerulean x 1, Cinnamon x 1, Abyssinian x 22, Huckleberry x 1, Abyssinian x 1, Cinnamon x 3, Abyssinian x 1, Huckleberry x 1, Cerulean x 2

▶ Row 48: Huckleberry x 3, Abyssinian x 1, Cinnamon x 4, Abyssinian x 23, Cinnamon x 1, Cerulean x 1

◀ Row 49: Cinnamon x 1, Canyon x 1, Abyssinian x 27, Huckleberry x 4

▶ Row 50: Abyssinian x 31, Canyon x 1, Cinnamon x 1

◀ Row 51: Canyon x 1, Cinnamon x 1, Abyssinian x 22, Huckleberry x 4, Abyssinian x 5

CORNER *(decrease at beginning of each row)*

▶ Row 52 [WS]: Cinnamon x 4, Abyssinian x 1, Huckleberry x 3, Abyssinian x 22, Cinnamon x 1, Canyon x 1

◀ Row 53 [RS]: Cinnamon x 1, Cerulean x 1, Abyssinian x 22, Cerulean x 2, Huckleberry x 1, Abyssinian x 1, Cinnamon x 3

▶ Row 54: Canyon x 2, Cinnamon x 1, Abyssinian x 1, Huckleberry x 1, Cerulean x 1, Abyssinian x 22, Cerulean x 1, Cinnamon x 1

◀ Row 55: Cerulean x 1, Huckleberry x 1, Abyssinian x 22, Cerulean x 1, Huckleberry x 1, Abyssinian x 1, Cinnamon x 1, Canyon x 1

▶ Row 56: Canyon x 1, Cinnamon x 1, Abyssinian x 1, Huckleberry x 1, Abyssinian x 22, Huckleberry x 1, Cerulean x 1

◀ Row 57: Huckleberry x 2, Abyssinian x 22, Huckleberry x 1, Abyssinian x 1, Cinnamon x 1

▶ Row 58: Cinnamon x 1, Abyssinian x 23, Huckleberry x 2

◀ Row 59: Huckleberry x 2, Abyssinian x 23

▶ Row 60: Abyssinian x 22, Cerulean x 2

◀ Row 61: Cerulean x 2, Abyssinian x 21

▶ Row 62: Abyssinian x 20, Cinnamon x 2

◀ Row 63: Cinnamon x 2, Abyssinian x 19

▶ Row 64: Abyssinian x 18, Canyon x 2

◀ Row 65: Canyon x 2, Abyssinian x 17

▶ **Row 66:** Abyssinian x 16, Cinnamon x 2

◀ **Row 67:** Cinnamon x 2, Abyssinian x 15

▶ **Row 68:** Abyssinian x 14, Cerulean x 2

◀ **Row 69:** Cerulean x 2, Abyssinian x 13

▶ **Row 70:** Abyssinian x 12, Huckleberry x 2

◀ **Row 71:** Huckleberry x 2, Abyssinian x 11

▶ **Row 72:** Abyssinian x 10, Cerulean x 2

◀ **Row 73:** Cerulean x 2, Abyssinian x 9

▶ **Row 74:** Abyssinian x 8, Cinnamon x 2

◀ **Row 75:** Cinnamon x 2, Abyssinian x 7

▶ **Row 76:** Abyssinian x 6, Canyon x 2

◀ **Row 77:** Canyon x 2, Abyssinian x 5

▶ **Row 78:** Abyssinian x 4, Cinnamon x 2

◀ **Row 79:** Cinnamon x 2, Abyssinian x 3

▶ **Row 80:** Abyssinian x 2, Cerulean x 2

◀ **Row 81:** Cerulean x 2, Abyssinian x 1

▶ **Row 82:** Huckleberry x 2

◀ **Row 83:** Huckleberry x 1

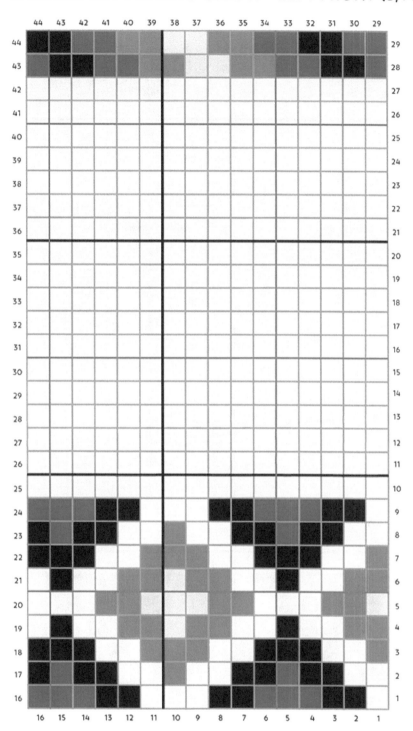

Quince & Co Owl – Abyssinian

Quince & Co Owl – Canyon

Quince & Co Owl – Cerulean

Quince & Co Owl – Cinnamon

Quince & Co Owl – Huckleberry

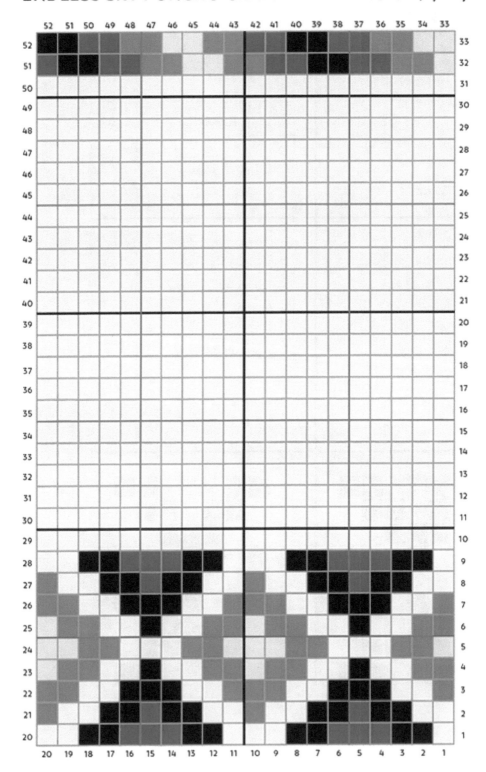

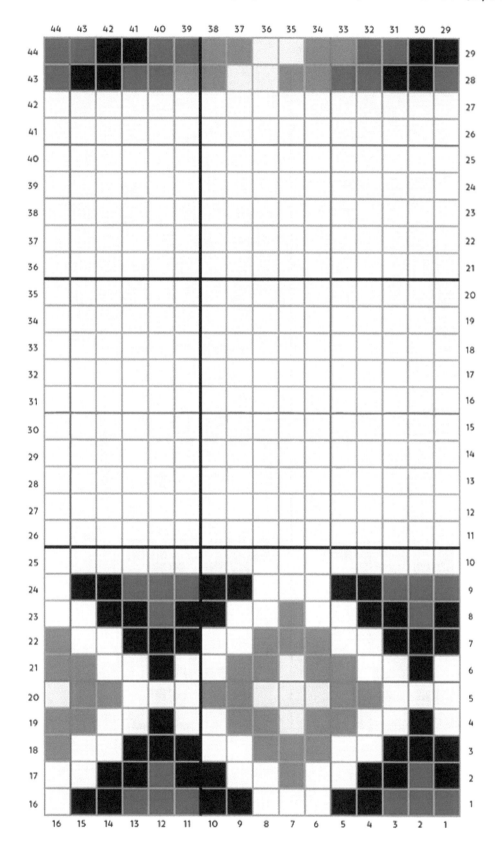

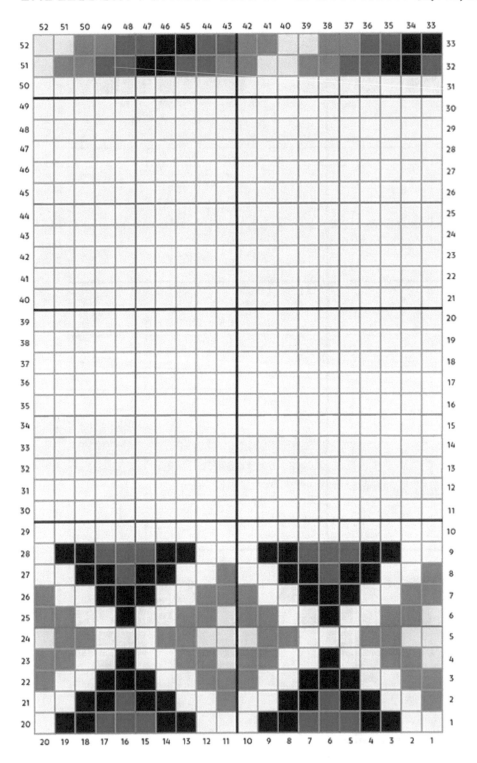

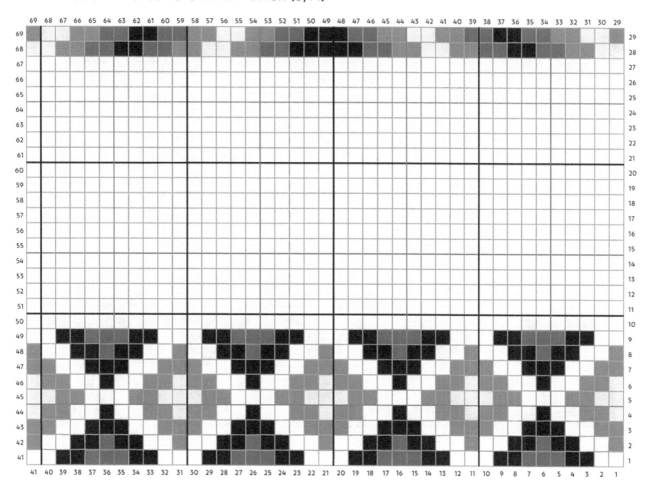

ENDLESS SKY PONCHO GRAPH – BACK (L/XL/2XL)

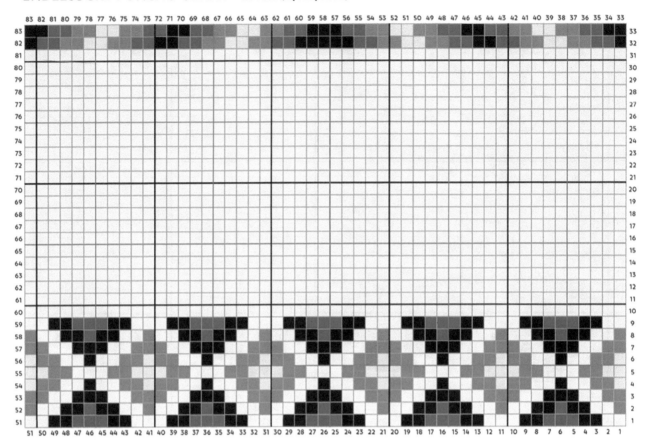

SEDIMENT BLANKET
PONCHO

While making a garment using the C2C technique may seem intimidating, this poncho is constructed from four basic rectangles that are puzzled together into a stylish multi-seasonal piece. Because this yarn gently transitions color on its own, you'll be free from managing any color changes and left with very few ends to weave in.

Difficulty Rating

Yarn

Lion Brand Scarfie (78% acrylic, 22% wool), 5 bulky (12/14-ply/chunky), 150g (311yd/285m), in the following shade:

› Ochre/Navy (203); 5 (6) skeins

Supplies

Size K (6.5mm) hook

Size H (5mm) hook

Size G (4mm) hook

Stitch markers or safety pins

Measurements and Sizing

Women's sizes: S/M (L/XL)

Fits bust: 34-40in/42-48in (86.25-101.5cm/107-122cm)

Finished measurements (excluding collar): 35 x 28in/39 x 30in (89 x 71cm/99 x 76cm)

Gauge (Tension)

4 tiles measure $3^{1}/_{2}$in (9cm) using size K (6.5mm) hook and Lion Brand Scarfie

Stitch

Double crochet (UK treble crochet) C2C

NOTES

◢ *To customize the size of your poncho, add or remove rows from your main rectangles. If substituting yarn of a different weight, just work as many tiles necessary to meet the measurements of each rectangle listed below.*

Each front rectangle measures: S/M: $17^1/_2$ x 25in (44.5 x 63.5cm)
L/XL: 20 x $25^1/_2$in (51 x 65cm)

Each back rectangle measures: S/M: $17^1/_2$ x 28in (44.5 x 71cm) L/XL: 20 x 30in (51 x 76cm)

◢ *If you're using Lion Brand Scarfie yarn, be mindful to begin the front two rectangles from the same point in the yarn's color changes so as to create a somewhat symmetrical look in your poncho (repeat this with the back rectangles, although they do not need to match the front).*

◢ *If using a solid-colored yarn, you may choose to just work one large rectangle for the front and one large rectangle for the back. To do this, multiply the width of the graph x 2. Do not change rectangle height.*

Instructions

TO MAKE THE PONCHO

› Follow the written pattern and graph to make 2 front rectangles and 2 back rectangles.

› For joining (all sizes), pieces technically have no right or wrong side, so choose the best looking sides and designate them RS.

› Lay front rectangles flat WS facing up. Place long edges together to create the appearance of an arrow pointed downwards. With a strand of main color yarn and a tapestry needle, use seaming technique (see General Techniques: Joining C2C Pieces) to join front rectangles along long sides. Repeat same process with back rectangles.

› Lay joined front piece on top of joined back piece. Using stitch markers or safety pins, pin shoulder edges together. Seam as with rectangles from outer shoulder edge toward center. Stop with eight tiles remaining from center. Repeat on second shoulder. Sixteen total tiles should be left unseamed on both the front and back to create neck opening.

› Turn poncho right side out and continue with neck:

› For Neck (all sizes), attach yarn at center back seam. Work in the round with RS facing out. With size H hook:

Round 1: Ch 1, work 78 sc evenly around neck opening, slst to first sc of round to join. (78 sts)

Rounds 2-8: Ch 1, sc through the back loop only in each sc, slst to first sc of round to join.

Switch tosize G hook and continue:

Rounds 9-23: Repeat Round 2.

Round 24: Ch 1, slst through the back loop only in each sc, slst to first slst of round to join. Fasten off.

› For Border (all sizes), attach yarn anywhere around outer edge of poncho. Work one round of single crochet border (see General Techniques: Single Crochet Border) around entire body of poncho. Fasten off.

› Weave in remaining ends.

Pattern

FRONT (ALL SIZES)

◀ **Row 1 [RS]:** Navy x 1

▶ **Row 2 [WS]:** Navy x 2

◀ **Row 3:** Navy x 3

▶ **Row 4:** Navy x 4

◀ **Row 5:** Navy x 5

▶ **Row 6:** Navy x 6

◀ **Row 7:** Navy x 7

▶ **Row 8:** Navy x 8

◀ **Row 9:** Navy x 9

▶ **Row 10:** Navy x 10

◀ **Row 11:** Navy x 11

▶ **Row 12:** Navy x 12

◀ **Row 13:** Navy x 13

▶ **Row 14:** Navy x 14

◀ **Row 15:** Navy x 15

▶ **Row 16:** Navy x 16

◀ **Row 17:** Navy x 17

▶ **Row 18:** Navy x 18

◀ **Row 19:** Navy x 19

▶ **Row 20:** Navy x 20

Proceed with instructions for specific size below:

FRONT (S/M), CONT.

CORNER *(increase at beginning of RS rows, decrease at beginning of WS rows)*

◀ **Row 21 [RS]:** Navy x 20

▶ **Row 22 [WS]:** Navy x 20

◀ **Row 23:** Navy x 20

▶ **Row 24:** Navy x 20

◀ **Row 25:** Navy x 20

▶ **Row 26 :** Navy x 20

◀ **Row 27:** Navy x 20

▶ **Row 28:** Navy x 20

CORNER *(decrease at beginning of each row)*

◀ **Row 29 [RS]:** Navy x 19

▶ **Row 30 [WS]:** Navy x 18

◀ **Row 31:** Navy x 17

▶ **Row 32:** Navy x 16

◀ **Row 33:** Navy x 15

▶ **Row 34:** Navy x 14

◀ **Row 35:** Navy x 13

▶ **Row 36:** Navy x 12

◀ **Row 37:** Navy x 11

▶ **Row 38:** Navy x 10

◀ **Row 39:** Navy x 9

▶ **Row 40:** Navy x 8

◀ **Row 41:** Navy x 7

▶ **Row 42:** Navy x 6

◀ **Row 43:** Navy x 5

▶ **Row 44:** Navy x 4

◀ **Row 45:** Navy x 3

▶ **Row 46:** Navy x 2

◀ **Row 47:** Navy x 1

FRONT (L/XL), CONT.

◀ **Row 21 [RS]:** Navy x 21

▶ **Row 22 [WS]:** Navy x 22

◀ **Row 23:** Navy x 23

CORNER *(increase at beginning of all RS rows, decrease at beginning of all WS rows)*

▶ **Row 24 [WS]:** Navy x 23

◀ **Row 25 [RS]:** Navy x 23

▶ **Row 26 :** Navy x 23

◀ **Row 27:** Navy x 23

▶ **Row 28:** Navy x 23

◀ **Row 29:** Navy x 23

▶ **Row 30:** Navy x 23

CORNER *(decrease at beginning of all rows)*

◀ **Row 31 [RS]:** Navy x 22

▶ **Row 32 [WS]:** Navy x 21

◀ **Row 33:** Navy x 20

▶ **Row 34:** Navy x 19

◀ **Row 35:** Navy x 18

▶ **Row 36:** Navy x 17

◀ **Row 37:** Navy x 16

▶ **Row 38:** Navy x 15

◀ **Row 39:** Navy x 14

▶ **Row 40:** Navy x 13

◀ **Row 41:** Navy x 12

▶ **Row 42:** Navy x 11

◀ **Row 43:** Navy x 10

▶ **Row 44:** Navy x 9

◀ **Row 45:** Navy x 8

▶ **Row 46:** Navy x 7

◀ **Row 47:** Navy x 6

▶ **Row 48:** Navy x 5

◀ **Row 49:** Navy x 4

▶ **Row 50:** Navy x 3

◀ **Row 51:** Navy x 2

▶ **Row 52:** Navy x 1

BACK (ALL SIZES)

◀ **Row 1 [RS]:** Navy x 1

▶ **Row 2 [WS]:** Navy x 2

◀ **Row 3:** Navy x 3

▶ **Row 4:** Navy x 4

◀ **Row 5:** Navy x 5

▶ **Row 6 :** Navy x 6

◀ **Row 7:** Navy x 7

▶ **Row 8:** Navy x 8

◀ **Row 9:** Navy x 9

▶ **Row 10:** Navy x 10

◀ **Row 11 :** Navy x 11

▶ **Row 12:** Navy x 12

◀ **Row 13:** Navy x 13

▶ **Row 14:** Navy x 14

◀ **Row 15:** Navy x 15

▶ **Row 16 :** Navy x 16

◀ **Row 17:** Navy x 17

▶ **Row 18:** Navy x 18

◀ **Row 19:** Navy x 19

▶ **Row 20:** Navy x 20

Proceed with instructions for specific size below:

BACK (S/M), CONT.

CORNER *(increase at beginning of RS rows, decrease at beginning of WS rows)*

◀ **Row 21 [RS]:** Navy x 20

▶ **Row 22 [WS]:** Navy x 20

◀ **Row 23:** Navy x 20

▶ **Row 24:** Navy x 20

◀ **Row 25:** Navy x 20

▶ **Row 26:** Navy x 20

◀ **Row 27:** Navy x 20

▶ **Row 28:** Navy x 20

◀ **Row 29:** Navy x 20

▶ **Row 30:** Navy x 20

◀ **Row 31:** Navy x 20

▶ **Row 32:** Navy x 20

CORNER *(decrease at beginning of each row)*

◀ **Row 33 [RS]:** Navy x 19

▶ **Row 34 [WS]:** Navy x 18

◀ **Row 35:** Navy x 17

▶ **Row 36:** Navy x 16

◀ **Row 37:** Navy x 15

▶ **Row 38:** Navy x 14

◀ **Row 39:** Navy x 13

▶ **Row 40:** Navy x 12

◀ **Row 41:** Navy x 11

▶ **Row 42:** Navy x 10

◀ **Row 43:** Navy x 9

▶ **Row 44:** Navy x 8

◀ **Row 45:** Navy x 7

▶ **Row 46:** Navy x 6

◀ **Row 47:** Navy x 5

▶ **Row 48:** Navy x 4

◀ **Row 49:** Navy x 3

▶ **Row 50:** Navy x 2

◀ **Row 51:** Navy x 1

BACK (L/XL), CONT.

◀ **Row 21 [RS]:** Navy x 21

▶ **Row 22 [WS]:** Navy x 22

◀ **Row 23:** Navy x 23

CORNER *(increase at beginning of all RS rows, decrease at beginning of all WS rows)*

▶ **Row 24 [WS]:** Navy x 23

◀ **Row 25 [RS]:** Navy x 23

▶ **Row 26:** Navy x 23

◀ **Row 27:** Navy x 23

▶ **Row 28:** Navy x 23

◀ **Row 29:** Navy x 23

▶ **Row 30:** Navy x 23

◀ **Row 31:** Navy x 23

▶ **Row 32:** Navy x 23

◀ **Row 33:** Navy x 23

▶ **Row 34:** Navy x 23

CORNER *(decrease at beginning of each row)*

◀ **Row 35 [RS]:** Navy x 22

▶ **Row 36 [WS]:** Navy x 21

◀ **Row 37:** Navy x 20

▶ **Row 38:** Navy x 19

◀ **Row 39:** Navy x 18

▶ **Row 40:** Navy x 17

◀ **Row 41:** Navy x 16

▶ **Row 42:** Navy x 15

◀ **Row 43:** Navy x 14

▶ **Row 44:** Navy x 13

◀ **Row 45:** Navy x 12

▶ **Row 46:** Navy x 11

◀ **Row 47:** Navy x 10

▶ **Row 48:** Navy x 9

◀ **Row 49:** Navy x 8

▶ **Row 50:** Navy x 7

◀ **Row 51:** Navy x 6

▶ **Row 52:** Navy x 5

◀ **Row 53:** Navy x 4

▶ **Row 54:** Navy x 3

◀ **Row 55:** Navy x 2

▶ **Row 56:** Navy x 1

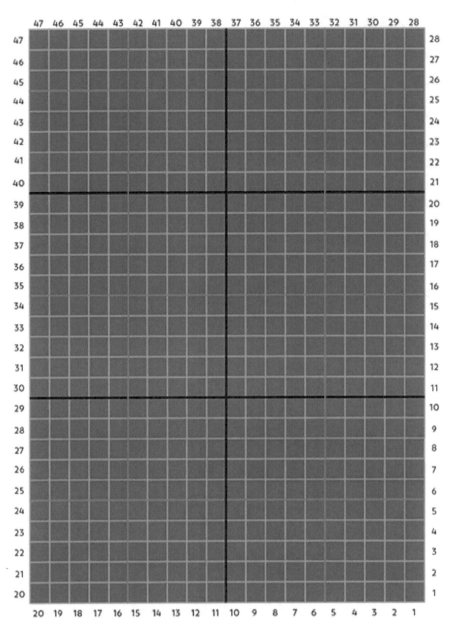

Lion Brand Scarfie – Ochre/Navy

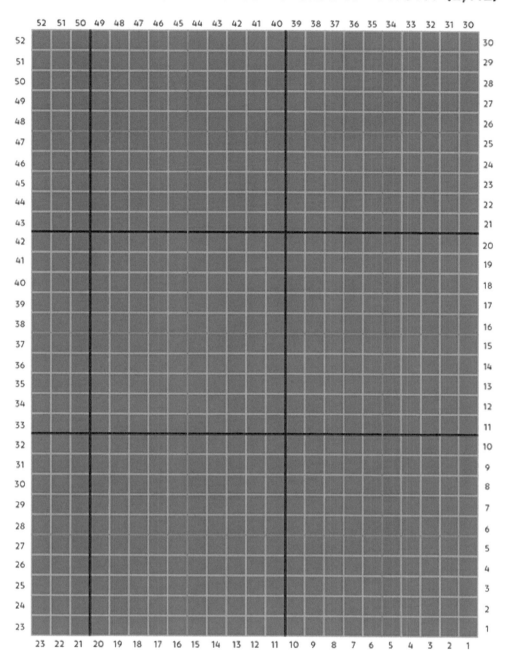

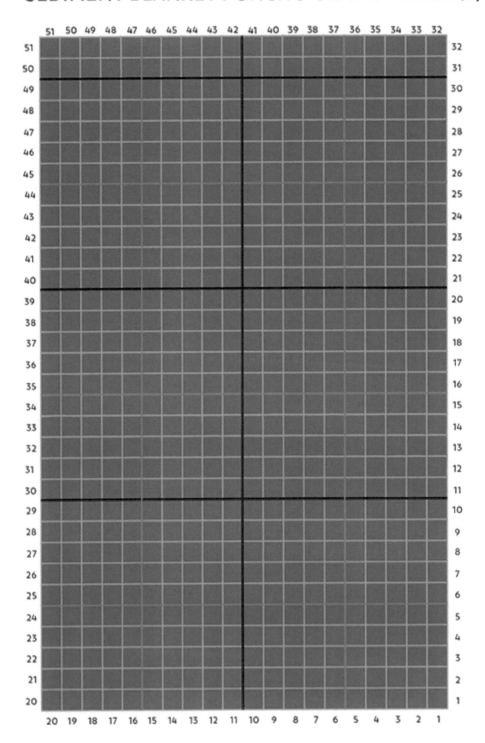

SEDIMENT BLANKET PONCHO GRAPH – BACK (L/XL)

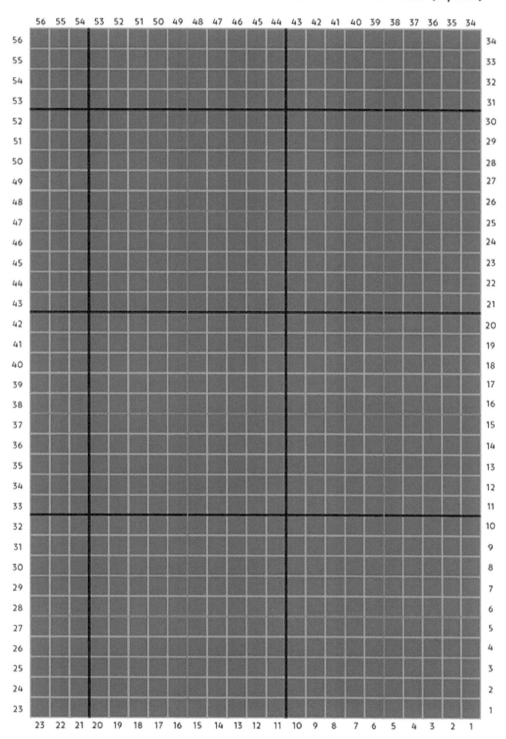

Techniques

Crochet Basics

US AND UK TERMINOLOGY

Be aware that crochet terms in the US differ from those in the UK. The crochet patterns in this book are written in US terms, but if you are used to working with UK terms here is a useful conversion chart to explain the difference:

US Term	UK Term
Single Crochet (sc)	Double Crochet (dc)
Half Double Crochet (hdc)	Half Treble Crochet (htr)
Double Crochet (dc)	Treble Crochet (tr)

ABBREVIATIONS

> **ch** – CHAIN

> **cont** – CONTINUED

> **dc** – DOUBLE CROCHET

> **dec** – DECREASE

> **hdc** – HALF DOUBLE CROCHET

> **inc** – INCREASE

> **RS** – RIGHT SIDE

> **sc** – SINGLE CROCHET

> **slst** – SLIP STITCH

> **sk** – SKIP

> **sp** – SPACE

> **WS** – WRONG SIDE

SLIP STITCH

Insert hook into stitch from front to back, yarn over and draw through all loops on hook.

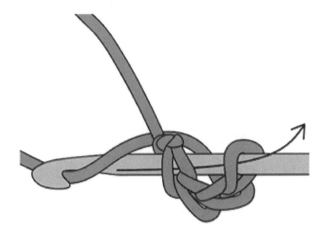

CHAIN

Yarn over and draw through loop on hook.

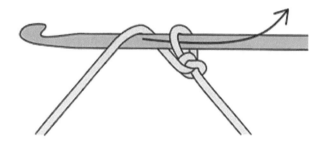

SINGLE CROCHET

Insert hook into stitch from front to back, yarn over and draw through stitch (2 loops on hook).

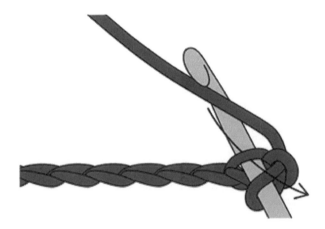

Yarn over and draw through both loops on hook (1 loop remains on hook).

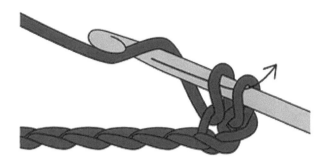

HALF DOUBLE CROCHET

Yarn over, insert hook into stitch from front to back, yarn over and draw through stitch (3 loops on hook).

Yarn over and draw through all three loops on hook (1 loop remains on hook).

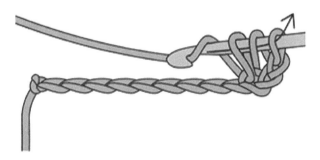

DOUBLE CROCHET

Yarn over, insert hook into stitch from front to back, yarn over and draw through stitch (3 loops on hook).

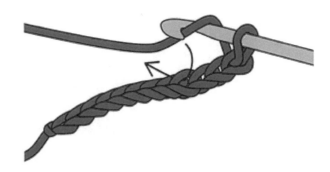

Yarn over and draw through first two loops on hook only (2 loops remain on hook).

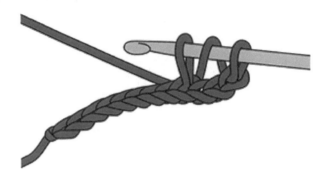

Yarn over and draw through both loops on hook (1 loop remains on hook).

General Techniques

FINISHING OFF A RAW EDGE OF DOUBLE CROCHET C2C

This technique is used to complete the Brushstrokes Scarf.

Step 1: Slst 4 along top edge of final C2C tile.

Step 2: [Sc, hdc, dc] in ch-3 of same tile.

Step 3: Slst 1 in ch-3 of next tile.

Repeat Steps 2 and 3 until end of row, ending with a slst in last tile of row.

4

SINGLE CROCHET BORDER

This simple border can serve as the foundational border on any C2C project. Once completed, a more decorative border can be added in subsequent rounds if desired.

Attach yarn, with a slst, in between any two tiles.

Step 1: Ch 1, sc in same sp between 2 tiles.

1

Step 2: Ch 2, sk tile.

Step 3: Sc in next sp between tiles.

Step 4: At corners, work 2 sc into corner point.

4

Repeat Steps 2-3, working corners as described above.
At end of round, ch 2 and slst to first sc of round to join.

CRAB STITCH BORDER (REVERSE SINGLE CROCHET)

The crab stitch is worked exactly like a typical single crochet stitch. The only difference is the direction in which it's crocheted.

When working a crab stitch border into a single crochet border, place 1 crab stitch in each sc and 2 crab stitches in each ch-2 sp.

Step 1: Join yarn with a slst in between any 2 tiles.

Step 2: Right-Handed – Insert hook in st to the right (instead of to left as usual). Left-Handed – Insert hook in st to the left (instead of to right as usual).

Step 3: Yarn over.

Step 4: Pull yarn through stitch. 2 loops on hook.

Step 5: Yarn over and pull through 2 loops on hook. 1 crab stitch is complete.

Repeat Steps 2-5.

Right-Handed Crab Stitch

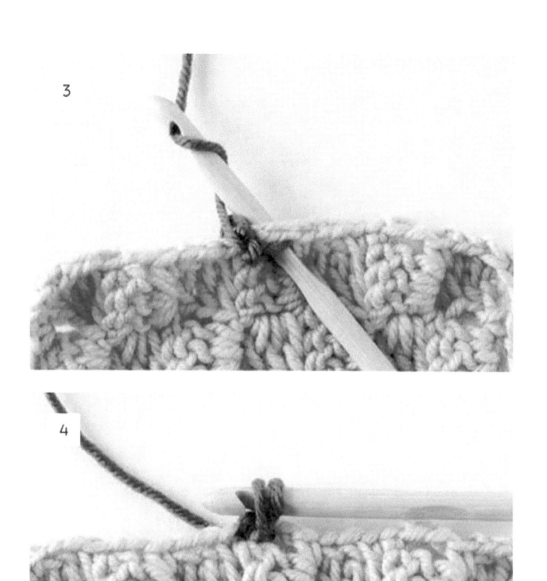

Left-Handed Crab Stitch

3

4

JOINING C2C PIECES

Seaming with this simple technique can often create the most inconspicuous joins between C2C tiles.

Lay work out flat with wrong sides facing up. Take care to align C2C tiles on each side. Where applicable, begin seam from bottom/outer edge of pieces.

Step 1: On right piece, insert tapestry needle from underneath side to top. Pull yarn through.

Step 2: On left piece, insert tapestry needle from underneath side to top. Pull yarn through.

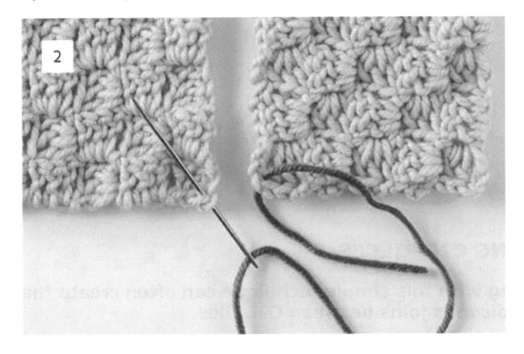

Repeat Steps 1 and 2 until seam is complete.

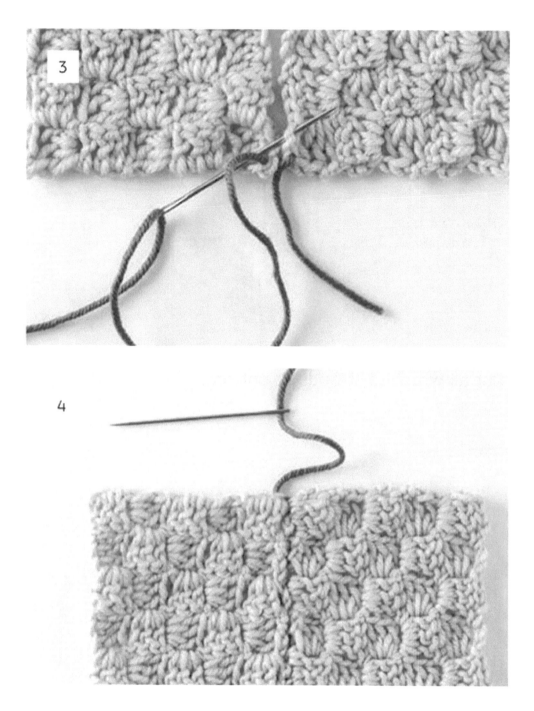

MAKING A TASSEL

Use a tassel maker or a piece of cardboard to make a tassel of any length.

Step 1: With a 10in (25cm) piece of yarn lying perpendicular underneath, wrap yarn around vertically and tie a knot in top of 10in (25cm) piece.

1

Step 2: Cut all wrapped strands at bottom.

2

Step 3: Tie a second 10in (25cm) piece of yarn around upper tassel to create a "bulb". Use crochet hook to pull those tails into middle of tassel.

3

Step 4: (Optional) To create a chunky tassel, tie an additional strand of yarn around tassel to create a second bulb. Use crochet hook to pull those tails into middle of tassel.

4

Trim tassel bottom so all strands are approximately the same length.

Use the knotted strands at the top of the tassel to attach it to your project. Once fastened on, pull fastening strands through bulb(s) and out bottom of tassel to disguise them. Trim again if necessary.

ADDING FRINGE

Step 1: Insert hook through RS of fabric.

Step 2: Pull strands through to form a loop.

Step 3: Pull strands of fringe through loop.

3

Step 4: Pull to tighten.

4

Repeat Steps 1-4.

MATTRESS STITCH

Step 1: Insert needle from left to right through the top loop only.

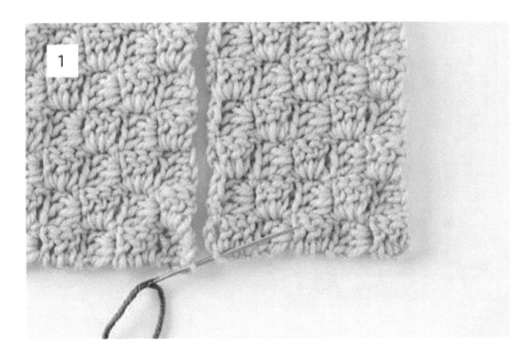

Step 2: Insert needle from right to left in next stitch in right panel and continue back into first stitch in left panel.

Step 3: Insert needle from left to right in next stitch in left panel and continue back into previous stitch in right panel.

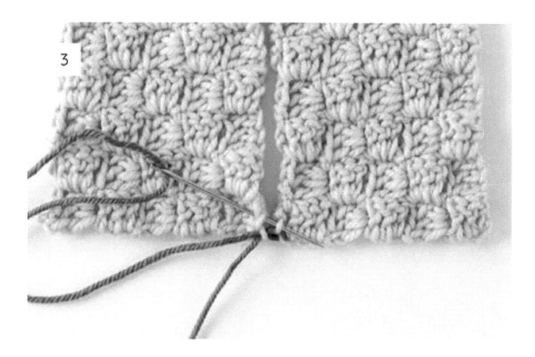

Repeat Steps 2 and 3 until seam is complete.

5